Border
Wanderings

THE MILL-POND
NEWCASTLE

Border
Wanderings

Local and Social History of the Marches

by

A T D EVANS

"BEST WISHES"

PHOTOGRAPHIC STUDIES
(1906 – 1935)

by

ROBERT NEWTON HEYWORTH
OF KNIGHTON

To the Past and the Future:
David Evans, My Grandfather (1877-1953)
Esme, Age 5, My Granddaughter

Published in 2008
by A T D Evans
Clun, Shropshire

© A T D Evans 2008

A CIP record for this book is available from
the British Library
ISBN 978-0-9560569-0-0

Printed in England by Craven Design and Print Ltd

Contents

Postcard History

Some believe, the life of the postcard began when Dr Emanuel Hermann of Vienna sent his correspondence on cards, around 1868. They were first used in Britain in 1870. The first coloured and illustrated cards were produced in British Heligoland in 1876. Then, in 1889, the French celebrated the Revolution with illustrated cards of the Eiffel Tower. By the 1890s, thick hotel-publicity cards were being used to advertise their establishments. Small pictorial vignette cards soon arrived. These had a small picture on the one side, with room for a short message on the other. Only the address and postal information could be used on the reverse side.

On 1st September 1894, the British Post Office granted permission for privately printed postcards, with a half penny adhesive stamp attached. The first picture postcards were not actual photographs; they were images taken from photographs or line drawings. It was in 1902 that the divided-back postcard came on the scene. On the one side a central line divided the address from the message, leaving the reverse of the card free for an illustration. From 1900 onwards, the 'real-photographic' picture postcards appeared in ever-increasing numbers. These were actual photograph prints, produced from negatives directly onto photographic paper that was postcard sized, usually five-and-a-half inches by three-and-a-half inches.

The fact that messages on attractive illustrated cards could be sent through the post for only half a penny, with up to seven deliveries a day, was irresistible. It started a craze that continued for the next two decades. You could send your message to an address in a nearby town one evening, confidently advising of your arrival the next morning! Worldwide, there were approximately 140 billion cards posted between 1900 and 1920. During that period, the quality of the 'real-photographic' picture postcard was of an exceptionally high standard. Soon, deltiology (the collecting of postcards) became the number one hobby in Great Britain. Queen Victoria was an avid collector, but only saw the early years of these postcards. Many of these 'real-photographic' postcards bore images taken with early plate-cameras that many believe produced pictures much superior to some taken today.

A T D Evans

New Postal Rates.

INLAND, FOREIGN & COLONIAL.

Rates in Force on and after
Midnight 12th-13th June, 1921.

INLAND POST.	FOREIGN & COLONIAL POST.
Letter Rate (unchanged).	Letters.
Not exceeding 3oz. in weight .. 2d.	(1) For the British Empire, the United States of America, Tangier, and H.M. Forces serving abroad:—
For every additional 1oz. or fraction of 1oz. .. .. ½d.	For first oz. .. .. 2d.
Postcard Rate.	For each additional oz. 1½d.
For every postcard .. .. 1½d.	(2) For all other places abroad:—
„ „ reply postcard .. 3d.	For first oz. .. .. 3d.
Printed Paper Rate	For each additional oz. 1½d.
Not exceeding 2oz. in weight .. 1d.	Postcards .. .. .. 1½d.
For each additional 2oz. or fraction of 2oz. up to 2lb. .. .. ½d.	Reply Postcards .. .. 3d.
Newspaper Rate (unchanged).	Printed Papers .. 1d. per 2 oz.
One penny for every copy not exceeding 6oz. in weight, with a further charge of one halfpenny for every additional 6 oz. or fraction of 6 oz.	Commercial Papers.
	For every 2 oz. .. .. 1d.
	with a minimum charge of 3d.
Parcel Rate (unchanged).	Samples.
Not exceeding 2 lb. in weight .. 9d.	For every 2 oz. .. .. 1d.
Exceeding 2 lb. but not exceeding 5 lb. 1/-	with a minimum charge of 2d.
„ 5 lb. „ „ 8 lb. 1/3	Registration Fee .. .. 3d.
„ 8 lb. „ „ 11 lb. 1/6	Advice of Delivery of
Registration Fee	Registered Articles .. 3d.
For every article registered .. 3d.	Insurance Fee.
The fees for insurance have been raised by adding 1d. at each point of the scale.	5d. for first £12. 2d. for each addtional £12.
Advice of Delivery of	Insured Boxes.—Postage.
Registered Postal Packets.	For every 2 oz. .. .. 2d.
For every article .. .. .. 3d.	with a minimum charge of 6d.
Blind Literature Rate.	Express Delivery Fee. .. 6d.
Not exceeding 1 lb. in weight .. ½d.	Blind Literature Rate.
Exceeding 1 lb. but not exceeding 5 lb. 1d.	½d. per lb. up to 6½ lb. with a maximum of 3d.
„ 5 lb. „ „ 6½ lb. 2d.	Canadian Magazine Post.
	No change

40

Foreword

Collecting the topographical postcards shown on the following pages has been challenging. Heyworth cards are becoming much more difficult to find and the prices asked can sometimes be prohibitive. However, in the process, I have met many fellow collectors and amateur local historians, who have freely imparted their accumulated knowledge, given advice and offered me every encouragement.

The geographical area covered by this publication is limited, but this is more than compensated for by the high quality of Robert Newton Heyworth's work. Furthermore, the borderlands between England and Wales are packed with interest, high in scenic value, and full of subjects awaiting exposure. I have often been asked, "What are your favourite Heyworth images?" It is a difficult question to answer, but high on my list must be the wonderful social history subjects recorded long ago on glass plates. Robert Newton Heyworth provides a superb, comprehensive record of village shows, fêtes, sports days, civic occasions and celebratory parades.

I have received much guidance and help from countless sources. Many people have turned up trumps with excellent examples of the photographer's art, or have provided me with information surpassing my wildest dreams. In particular, I had great fun talking to (or rather listening to) the inhabitants of the Clun Valley and beyond. Their sense of recall proved to be marvellous, and their memories encyclopaedic.

It is to all these supportive individuals that I unreservedly offer a most sincere thank-you. There are too many to mention by name; however, I would highlight the generous help furnished by the Leintwardine History Society: their archives and publications proved invaluable, and without them this publication would have been that much poorer. Special thanks to LHS Chairman, John Williams, and Secretary, Pam Hatherly. I am also appreciative of the considerate guidance given by friend and fellow postcard collector, Derek Walley, on the presentation, format and layout of this book. My gratitude is also extended to members of the Shropshire Postcard Club (a friendly group which meets monthly at Bayston Hill Memorial Hall) for their various contributions and suggestions. Last but not least, Craven Design and Print who have been most helpful with the printing of this book.

Finally, my sincere thanks go to various living relatives of Robert Newton Heyworth, particularly those in Rochdale, Bewdley, Worcestershire, and in South Devon, who provided me with personal family details. Above all, they were able to search out a portrait of the illustrious gentleman. This was no mean achievement, for he did spend most of his life on the other side of the camera lens!

Development of the Camera

The birth of the camera probably goes back to the 10th century when an Iraqi scholar, Ibn al-Haytham, found that a dark box with a pinhole in the end would throw an inverted image on the opposite wall. This is known as a *camera obscura*, from the Latin for *dark room*. It was much later, in the 1500s, that the Italians introduced the lens to replace the pinhole. A lens is an optical device which transmits and refracts light, and produces an image of a distant object.

The word photography was first used by Sir John Herschel in 1839: derived from Greek *photos* which means light, and *graphiene* meaning to draw – hence the word photography, meaning *drawing with light.*

The first permanent photograph was made in 1827 by Frenchman Joseph Nicéphore Niépce, taking eight hours to expose. He used a sliding wooden box camera made by Frenchmen Vincent and Charles Chevalier.

Joseph then teamed up with fellow countryman Louis Jacques Mandé Daguerre to develop photographic plates that brought the exposure time down to less than 30 minutes. The image was made permanent by immersing it in salt. Joseph died during the development, and Louis named the invention the *daguerreotype* in 1839, and promptly sold the patent to the French government.

In 1833 William Henry Fox Talbot invented several new processes including a machine that based prints on light-sensitive paper, removing the need for bitumen or copper paper. It was in 1851 that another Englishman, Frederick Scott Archer, introduced his *wet collodion process* which reduced the exposure time to three seconds. He used a mixture of collodion and potassium iodide immersed in a solution of silver nitrate. Although successful, the wet plates were difficult for travelling photographers to handle. This problem was rectified by Dr Richard Maddox in 1871; he used the recently discovered *gelatin* (an animal by-product) to produce an emulsion that would spread on a glass plate. The *gelatin dry plate* was born.

Hermann Wilhelm Vogel, a German professor, discovered in 1873 that treating collodion emulsion plates with aniline dyes made them sensitive to the colours absorbed by the dyes – the birth of colour photography.

In 1878, Englishman Charles Bennett, produced a new gelatin dry plate which reduced exposure time dramatically.

Alex Parkes from Birmingham invented celluloid in 1861, and Henry Reichenbach developed transparent flexible celluloid for the American George Eastman, founder of the famous Eastman Kodak Company, which brought photography to the masses.

Many more inventors, developers and chemicals were involved in bringing photography up to the status it enjoys today – far too many to mention, but they all played their part. The journey from birth to fruition has been a real United Nations effort, culminating in the new world of digital photography.

Introduction

Many local history publications use postcards and photographic material to illustrate their particular subject matter. Almost without exception there is a glaring failure to acknowledge the expertise of the photographer responsible for what are often quite exceptional images. Feeling strongly about this omission, and as a recent convert to the charms of the Edwardian postcard – my baptism being in 2002 – this account is intended primarily to celebrate the life and artistic vision of one truly professional photographer. As my postcard collection grew apace, I realised that the superior examples of my indigenous area of South West Shropshire were those taken by one particular master photographer: that man was Robert Newton Heyworth of Broad Street, Knighton, Radnorshire – now part of Powys.

Above all else, this compilation is designed to show the early professional photographer at his best, irrespective of his chosen subject. High-class equipment and superior camera technique were just the starting points; Mr Heyworth appears to have exercised strict, almost fussy, control over the dark-room side of production. After all, the finished article was not to be spoilt by faulty developing of the negative by either himself, or a member of his staff. It is indeed rare to find a Heyworth image which has failed to stand the test of time; the light-sensitive emulsion finish and the highly important need for contrast always appear to have been maintained. This book is, therefore, a pictorial history, which wholeheartedly acknowledges and underlines the endeavours of one very notable photographer.

I soon became aware of many of Heyworth's characteristic 'marks', for example the conjoined 'HK' at the bottom of some images. His writing was also distinctive, and his picture captions invariably have a squiggly line to the front and rear. Familiarity enabled me to identify Heyworth's work, even if he had omitted to provide an explanatory legend to the postcard. His work has a certain recognisable individuality, best illustrated by his ability to turn what appears to be a quite ordinary scene into a picture of much beauty. He was a skilful operator, with an innate ability to make the most of any setting or location.

We are fortunate that 'my good friend', Mr Heyworth, and his camera travelled the length and breadth of the Clun Valley, North West Herefordshire and the Welsh Borderlands of Radnorshire. Virtually every community, large or small, attracted his roving lens: the village shop, the local smithy, the post office, the neighbourhood hostelry, the parish church, the wayside non-conformist chapel, the river bridge, the local landowner's mansion, the ruined castle and the much-prized animated street scene, all contribute to a remarkable photographic portfolio of life as it was a century ago. However, it would be remiss not to spotlight one particularly endearing trait, namely Heyworth's penchant for social gatherings. His recording of such events as peace celebrations, village sports days, garden parties, flower and agricultural shows, and church festivals are a superb archive of life in a past era. He considered such occasions worthy of his professional attention.

The remaining task was to find out as much as possible about our Mr Heyworth's family background, and to attempt to throw some light on his likely personality and any obvious motivating factors. It is hoped the accompanying text, researched for the past three years, from many different sources, will go some way to successfully supplementing the wonderful images provided by Robert Newton Heyworth, an extraordinary master photographer from the Golden Age.

A T D Evans
Clun, 2008.

Robert Newton Heyworth

1877 - 1935

The only advert found for Robert Newton Heyworth

About the Author

Albert Thomas David Evans (alias **A**ttention **t**o **D**etail Evans) was born at Hawkstone House, 14 Market Street, Craven Arms, on 26th October 1939, the second son of David and Nora Elizabeth (née Thomas) Evans. David comes from a family which in various capacities has been involved in commerce for generations. His father and grandfather were smallholders at Whettleton Hill, Stokesay, and both his great-grandfather and great-great-grandfather were coal merchants (Samuel Chester & Son) with depots at railway stations in the area. The business later became C W Summerfield, Coal Merchant and Builders' Merchant in Station Drive, Craven Arms.

At 15 David left school, having been educated at Stokesay Primary School, Church Stretton Secondary School and Shrewsbury Technical College. His father died in 1959 at the age of 52, leaving David to run the smallholding. A career shift in 1961 saw him opening a retail confectionery/greengrocery shop at the family home in Market Street, Craven Arms. Moving to 5,000sq ft premises at Lower Market Street in 1971, David switched to retailing hardware, gardening and DIY products under the business name of Davy's Outpost. In 1981, the firm became a wholesale enterprise, changed its name to Border Distribution, and moved to a new base at Long Lane Industrial Estate, Craven Arms. Retirement came in 1999.

Unaccustomed idleness was soon overcome by a blossoming interest in local history and collecting Edwardian postcards of his home county and surrounding area. This hobby has taken David all over the country to secondhand bookshops and car-boot sales, to junk shops, far-flung auctions, and of course to postcard fairs. One obvious consequence is the detail and enthusiasm evident in this publication.

David and his wife Beryl, who were married in 1966, first lived in Craven Arms, later moving to Hopesay where the family spent 27 happy years. Two years ago, they moved to a new home overlooking the castle ruins at Clun.

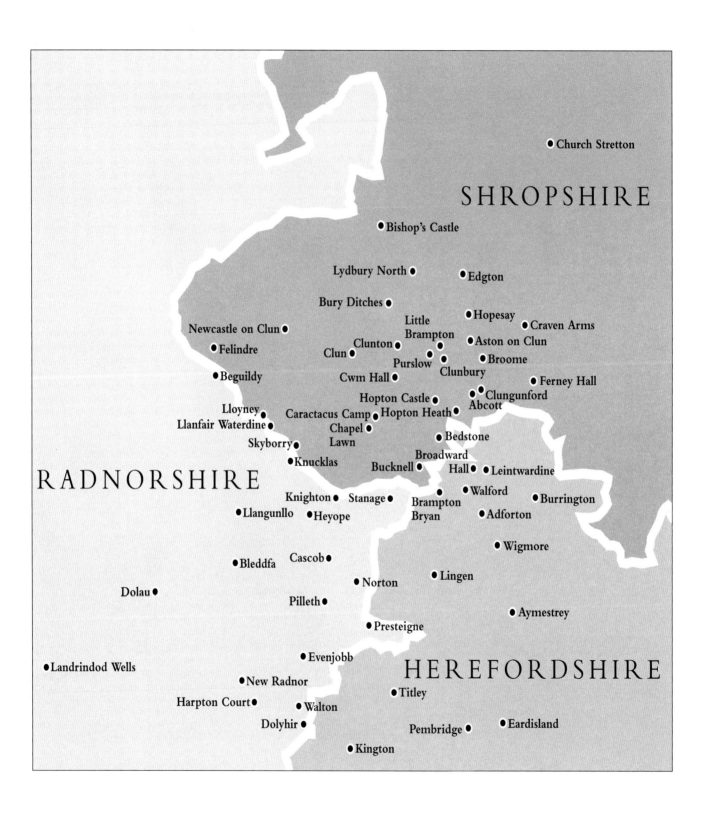

List of Towns and Villages

Robert Newton Heyworth composed this picture of his sister Janey's wedding to Rupert Clegg in 1910, rushed around the other side of the lense to be included on the extreme right.

Robert Newton Heyworth – Master Photographer
A Brief Account of his Family Life and Business Accomplishments

Robert Newton Heyworth came into this world on 28th August 1877, the first of three children born to Isaac and Emma Heyworth. Isaac was employed as a cotton operative – 'a beamer' and, aged 22, he married 19-year-old Emma Whipp, a woollen weaver and daughter of a coal miner, at Smallbridge Congregational Church, Rochdale on 13th April 1876. They went to live at 315 Halifax Road, Brickfield, Wuerdle, Rochdale. Robert's siblings were Florence, born 1882, and Jane (known as Janey), born 1888.

Little is known of Robert's early life, but on 11th September 1905, at the age of 28, he married 31-year-old Elizabeth Ellen Heaton, of Howarth Cross Street, Rochdale, at Smallbridge New Congregational Church, Rochdale and the couple set up home at 33 Prescott Street, Rochdale. It is believed Robert went to work with an uncle in a photographic business at Junction Studios, Drake Street, Rochdale, and he may possibly have spent a period of time as an employee of Renaud Studios of Chorlton cum Hardy. The evidence for this assumption is that a few early cards of the Knighton district utilise this photographer's printed backs. It must be assumed that Robert quickly acquired the necessary expertise in the art of photography, a profession still very much in its infancy in the early years of the 20th century.

In 1906 Robert and his new wife made a bold decision, and moved from industrialised central Lancashire to the rural tranquillity of the borderlands, the small market town of Knighton in Radnorshire, just a stone's throw across the English border. Robert must have had sufficient foresight to realise the commercial potential of this sparsely populated area. It is highly likely that he and Elizabeth Ellen had already visited the town, perhaps having seen an advertisement in the trade press or having heard of an established enterprise that was for sale.

In all probability, Robert took over the photographic studio of Edwin Debenham. There had been a photographer in West Street, Knighton, since at least 1891 when Richard William J Jones was the practitioner. It cannot be emphasised enough that Robert Newton Heyworth's timing was absolutely perfect. Maybe he was fortunate in finding suitable premises for his new venture, but he had the necessary vision to take advantage of the developing national enthusiasm for the picture postcard. By the start of the 20th century, the postcard had become the normal and accepted method of communication. By the outbreak of the First World War, 800 million cards were posted annually. These figures do not include postcards which went unused, or were placed directly into the family album.

The stage had been set for considerable expansion in business, a development entirely independent of the normal photographic studio workload. Photographers nationwide found themselves providing millions of images for the new picture postcards. Albeit on a relatively small patch in the English/Welsh borderlands, Robert Newton Heyworth obviously became a significant contributor in this helter-skelter for custom. The business prospered, and Mr Heyworth soon moved to a larger and more central studio at 21 Broad Street, Knighton; it is believed that further expansion followed shortly with the incorporation of premises at No 24, a studio operated by William Henry Lloyd since 1861.

In the early years, our relatively inexperienced and possibly cash-strapped practitioner confined himself to pedal power, using his bicycle to get around the surrounding hilly countryside. To this day, there are local residents who remember Robert, with his heavy tripod and camera slung over his back, using this mode of transport. One nonagenarian lady from Knighton vividly remembers seeing her local photographer cycling near Lloyney, some four miles north-west of the town. Apparently, Robert Newton Heyworth was here because he had been asked to take special anniversary pictures at Lloyney in 1915. He did not, however, neglect the bread-and-butter side of the business, for family portraiture had always provided a steady flow of customers. After all, the mass use of the Kodak Brownie box camera and the resultant proliferation of amateur snapshots was still a long way off. This situation gradually changed from the late 1920s onwards.

Sound business returns meant that Robert was able to invest in a motorbike and sidecar, enabling him to get around the countryside that much quicker. Above all, it allowed him to offer a highly efficient wedding service. Having taken the pictures at the local church or chapel, he was able to return post-haste to his studio dark-room, develop the negatives and so provide a folio of instant proofs a little later in the day at the reception. Competence and efficiency ultimately led to an increase in sales and enhanced his local reputation. One result was Robert's purchase of his first motor car in the early 1920s.

With his improved mobility, Robert was able to cast his photographic net that much wider. He motored into North West Herefordshire, to Brampton Bryan, Leintwardine and Adforton, followed by Wigmore, Lingen and Burrington, Kington and Eardisland, culminating in a trip to Pembridge which produced a wonderful selection of images. Day trips took him deep into Radnorshire, to New Radnor, Dolau, Llanbister, Llandrindod Wells and the Elan and Rhayader Valleys; and excursions into Shropshire as far as Church Stretton, Craven Arms and Edgton are also known to have taken place.

It seems that through his business contacts, Mr Heyworth became a much respected pillar of the community, described by one local resident as being "rather an artistic gentleman with long flowing locks." Curiously, one Radnor native remembers him for his brown fingers – caused not by nicotine, but by the chemicals used in his dark-room processes. It is by no means surprising to learn that Heyworth's studio portraits still adorn the walls of numerous homes in rural Radnorshire: family mementoes which have stood the test of time.

Notwithstanding this lucrative work, Robert Newton Heyworth can frequently be found pursuing his other interest, recording the regular fixtures of the social calendar in his area. His images captured much of rural life in the first two decades of the 20th century. In fact, his coverage appears comprehensive; every local event was registered by his camera, so much so that it is strongly suspected that organisers of any such occasion would ensure that he had received the necessary tip-off, or ventured to send him a special invitation, thus guaranteeing his attendance. As a result, most social gatherings ranging from the annual May Fair to the local flower and produce show, the squire's garden party, church festivals, the busy horse fair, World War I money-raising campaigns and, above all, the peace celebrations featured in Heyworth's schedule. This record, together with reminders of the numerous personalities of the period, prominent buildings, churches and chapels, village street scenes – of course without cars and street furniture – public houses, shops and post offices form a priceless archive of life 100 years ago. These photographs are often the only such material available to local historians, researchers and collectors alike, all of whom in their own individual way wish to chronicle the past.

Unfortunately, whilst business was progressing very satisfactorily, all was not well with family matters. It is known that Robert and Elizabeth had an infant boy, Bobby, living with them from about 1918 but, in spite of a thorough search of the national birth records, no trace can be found of his registration, a procedure, of course, that was required by law. Because of this fact, it has to be assumed that Bobby was adopted. Regrettably, the child had been born with a speech impediment. Absolute tragedy was to follow, for on 12th August 1920 Elizabeth Ellen Heyworth died at the early age of 45. She appears to have had many complications, all probably associated with tuberculosis, but the cause of death was chronic peritonitis. This left Robert Newton Heyworth with a serious domestic problem, bringing up a child who required some specialist care. Bobby attended Knighton Elementary School and his speech impairment obviously caused communication problems, especially in expressing himself. What is not known is whether his father sought permanent help with the child's upbringing. The answer must surely be affirmative, although research indicates that Bobby was a boarder at the Rhayader Institution for a while before he eventually started work as an agricultural labourer on several farms in the Rhayader district. It seems that Bobby was able to live a largely independent life, no doubt living-in with one or more farming families. It is of interest to note that in 1992 he met and recognised a Knighton resident whilst visiting the Horseshoe Pass, Llangollen. Incidentally, the author would appreciate any further information relating to this sad chapter.

That part of the business associated with the production of new images for picture postcards was to be seriously affected by a gradual but significant fall in interest in this form of communication. The increased availability of the telephone and the preference for a more confidential means of correspondence was to lead to postcards noticeably falling out of favour, a trend which started in the 1920s and continued into the 1930s. Improved mobility, more particularly enhanced transportation links, was also a contributory factor. In his later years Robert Newton Heyworth did not enjoy the best of health. It is understood that in the late 1930s he had some difficulty in keeping to his hitherto busy schedule; long working days and inclement weather only served to increase his frailty. Like his wife before him, he too was to succumb to tuberculosis, dying of this infectious disease in Offa Lodge, Knighton on 15th March 1935 at the age of 57. He was buried in the Municipal Cemetery in his home town of Rochdale on 19th March 1935. His gravestone epitaph *'Peace after Pain'* perhaps aptly summarises the family trials and tribulations experienced over several decades.

Precisely what happened to the Heyworth photographic business following Robert's death is uncertain. However, another local photographer, namely Percy Benzie Abery of nearby Builth Wells, does seem to have gained access to Heyworth's glass plates and negatives. It may well have been part of a business arrangement made between the two photographers when Heyworth realised that his health was failing. Corroboration of this theory has not been possible. Nevertheless, many of the postcards produced by Abery between the two World Wars are in fact Heyworth's work, easily identifiable by the distinctive form of lettering used in his captions. On reflection, it is a fair assumption that Abery did take over the Heyworth business at some juncture and re-cycled the prize images, though there is no specific attempt on Abery's part to personalise them as his own.

A truly high-class professional, an artistic man who totally understood the photographic business, Robert Newton Heyworth was an absolute perfectionist. We are deeply indebted to him for recording virtually everything of importance across a large swathe of the English/Welsh borderlands. His legacy is an unrivalled pictorial dossier, parts of which are unashamedly reproduced within the following pages. All photographs are the work of Robert Newton Heyworth.

2 cameras similar to the ones used by Robert Newton Heyworth

The Ancient Hundred – An Explanation

The establishment of boundaries was important to our ancestors. The British landscape is a network of what were territorial statements within a given framework, much of which dates back to Anglo-Saxon times. The divisions of the countryside utilised here are the groupings called 'hundreds'.

The 'shire', a late Anglo-Saxon period unit of administration, had a direct link to the central seat of government, for it was the sheriff – the 'shire reeve' – who acted as the representative for each shire. Within these county units, there developed before the Norman Conquest a system of intermediate territories, smaller than the county unit, but larger than the 'tithing' – roughly the equivalent of a civil parish. These 10th century intermediate districts were called hundreds over most of England and Wales. Their purpose was primarily that of a judicial unit, the hundred court being a district meeting held every four weeks at a fixed meeting place, hence The Hundred House, a name still frequently seen today.

The hundred sub-division was also responsible for collecting taxes, and it is a distinct possibility that the origin of the term lay in the fact that it was a designated area assessed as one hundred hides – a hide being an ancient way of apportioning land, approximately the equivalent of 100 acres, or as much land as could be tilled by one plough in a year.

Whilst these sub-divisions no longer have any standing in civil, ecclesiastical or judicial matters, they are helpful in providing a meaningful framework for the many subjects and places touched upon within this book. It may be of interest to know that Shropshire has 15 hundreds, Herefordshire 11 and Radnorshire 6, only some of which are relevant to the contents of the present publication.

A perfect example of a hundred house. This one is situated at Purslow in the Clun Valley.

Chapter One

The Hundred of Clun

Clun
Chapel Lawn
Newcastle on Clun
Llanfair Waterdine/Skyborry

1.1   Clun - Historically Engaging

THE VILLAGE SCHOOL   1908

The earliest recorded school in Clun was that held in the chamber over the north porch of St George's Church; classes were established here in the early 1800s. This seat of learning was later moved to the kitchen of the vicarage. Large by normal village standards, St George's C of E Elementary School was purpose-built in 1860 for 292 children. The number presently on roll is under 100. At the time of the photograph, the school was under the disciplinary control of Frank Short, ably assisted at different times by his daughters Florence and Emily.

THE MILL POND/CASTLE LAKE   1926

A rural idyll demanding the attention of any camera lens, but sadly a non-repeatable image! The stream-fed lake provided water for the nearby mill which is now a youth hostel. Soon after World War II, a businessman from Birmingham purchased the lake and decided to clear its weed-choked depths, to dredge and remove years of accumulated rubbish. Unfortunately he did not ask, and no-one thought to tell him that this body of water was man-made and clay-lined. The machines went in and the water went out, never to return! The depression was eventually filled, and at present part of the area is used as a football pitch. Much local debate currently centres round the possibility of restoring the lake to its former splendour, thereby recreating this pastoral scene of the 1920s.

THE ROYAL GEORGE   1914

This beer house, located at the junction of High Street and Ford Street, must have been a dwelling house when, early in the 19th century, John Hints purchased and converted the property for use as a Temperance Hotel. Subsequently, in the late-Victorian period, it changed its name to The Royal George and became licensed premises. Always referred to locally as The Ship, it was named after the fighting man-o'-war of that title which was launched on the Thames circa 1760. Of massive proportions, this early gunship was 175-foot long and its construction had required the felling of 60 acres of timber. The hostelry closed in the 1930s, changing its function yet again to that of refreshment rooms. It has now reverted back to its original use as a private residence. The Wesleyan Methodist Chapel to the rear was built in 1835.

THE COTTAGE HOSPITAL   1934

This building in the High Street started life as a Dower House for the Morris family of the Hurst Estate, and was known as Clun House. It was later purchased by Louisa Darell Brown of Hastings, who adapted the property and provided the necessary endowment for the foundation of St Catherine's Clun Valley Cottage Hospital. It was established in memory of her mother, Catherine Field, widow of Sir Henry Field and sister of the late Eliza Morris of The Hurst, who died on 8th October 1891. The hospital was dedicated and officially opened by the Right Rev James Atlay, Bishop of Hereford, on 11th October 1893. This building holds especially happy memories for the author and his wife whose son, David, was born here in 1968. The hospital closed in the 1970s and more recently has been totally refurbished and now houses several flats.

THE LETTER BOX OAK, OAK BANK   1906

Postman Fred Mold is seen arriving in his pony and trap to collect the day's mail from the postbox within the trunk of the oak tree. The tree was situated on the road to Anchor and was known locally as The Post Office Tree. It was probably unique. However, this ancient tree was later felled because of the fire risk associated with passing travellers and vagrants.

POST OFFICE AND STAFF, MARKET SQUARE   1907

A posed but, nevertheless, evocative record of how things were in the first decade of the 20th century. A quick roll-call identifies in the doorway assistant Gladys Cooke, Mr Lewis and Mrs Jessie Lewis, to their left by the head of the horse is Tom Francis from The Ferns, and Fred Mold holds the horse steady. On the left is Tom Pugh with his bicycle, then postman J Luther, and Mary Tudor with her father, Tom Tudor. The mail cart collected and delivered twice daily to Aston on Clun, and between times was busy delivering and collecting mail to and from other points in the area. Note the stand full of postcards for sale in the left-hand window, a display which would surely include numerous examples from the lens of Mr Heyworth.

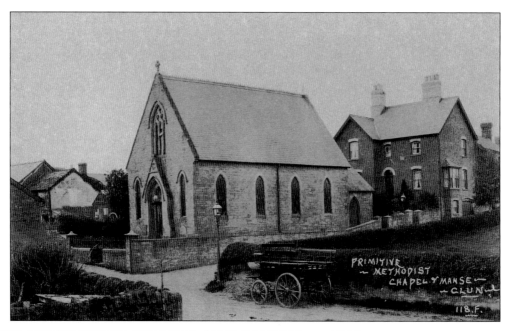

PRIMITIVE METHODIST CHAPEL AND MANSE   1910

Situated on the Craven Arms road, the chapel is still in use today although the manse is now a private house. The 'Prims' first came to Clun in 1828 and initially used private houses for their gatherings, at times holding open-air services. It was January 1835 before this prestigious chapel was opened, and by 1837 the Sunday School was flourishing with six teachers and 133 scholars. These so-called dissenters had at first not been well-received by many in the Established Church. Problems were at their worst from the middle of the 17th Century. Wounds started to heal after the passing of the Toleration Act of 1689, but spasmodic opposition continued until the non-conformists were able to build their own places of worship.

THE PARISH CHURCH OF ST GEORGE   1915

Built on a Saxon foundation, this large church has numerous Norman features, the most prominent being its sturdy, pyramidal west tower, capped by short timber bell-sections, all of a type found at other places in the borderlands. In its lofty and prominent position, perfect for the tending of its flock, it invites further inspection, and the visitor will not be disappointed. Much of the interior has an 11th or 12th century atmosphere; the arches in the north aisle and chancel, as well as the nave arcades, are all original and of this early period. Victorian restoration was carried out in 1873 and the gentleman architect responsible was the eminent G E Street. His work, particularly the belated restitution of Civil War damage, is of the highest order.

THE MARKET SQUARE, CLUN TO CRAVEN ARMS OMNIBUS   1919

Pure nostalgia! The Ludlow Motor Garage's Clun Valley motor service ran twice daily from Clun to Craven Arms. It must have been a great improvement on horse-drawn carriages. The vehicle advertises itself with a large emblem on its radiator top, a star indicating that it was built at Star Engineering Co in Wolverhampton. Bert Wood is identified as the driver; his passenger wearing the trilby hat is Arthur Morris from the Cottage Bakery, and sitting next to him is Arthur Stringer, the landlord of the Buffalo Hotel. The vehicle is parked outside the post office and all appears to be ready for the commencement of the eight-mile journey to Craven Arms.

THE MARKET SQUARE   1919

Everything is posed here. "No moving, please," would have been photographer Heyworth's last words. The Clun Valley Service bus stands outside Jessie Lewis's post office premises. Of course, not everyone will climb aboard this 14-seater, one lady though appears to be sure of her seat for she has her travel rug over her arm to keep her cosy during the journey. The Buffalo Hotel sign hangs above the numerous interested onlookers. Morris's bakery is in the far background and the premises of the London, City and Midland Bank are immediately behind the bus. To the right is Francis Sherwood's butcher's shop with its rather makeshift sunblind much in evidence.

THE REVELS, THE CASTLE GROUNDS   1922

Maypole dancing appears to have been popular at this time in Clun and the borderlands. The maypole and its complement of 15 dancers would have paraded around the streets on a horse-drawn dray and having reached the castle grounds, the intricate dancing encircling the maypole would begin. The lady standing to the left is probably Minnie Griffiths, daughter of the High Street butcher, for she undertook the task of training the girls over a number of years. Continual practice must have been essential to perfect the interweaving of the ribbons; just how all were neatly unravelled after being tightly bunched against the pole is quite remarkable! The girls were always uniformly dressed in white cotton dresses with ribbons in their hair.

PATRIOTIC SALE 1915

Another wonderful social history record! As with most other towns and villages, Clun did its bit to support the war effort and much time and energy was expended raising money at these self-styled 'patriotic sales' during World War I. This particular sale took place at Lower House farmyard in Clun. Lady Powis is seen opening the event together with the Rev Harold Scott, while other local dignitaries stand alongside. This sale was held on 8th September 1915 on a hot, sunny day judging by the number of parasols being used to shade their owners from the sun. Apparently, a good turnout could always be guaranteed, as could the sartorial elegance of all those present.

THE PARISH CHURCH – THE REFURBISHMENT OF THE BELLS 1914

St George's six bells had hung within their tower framework since the 16th century. There is no record of any work of significance being carried out over the succeeding 300 years. Following a survey, the parochial church council decided in the first decade of the 20th century that extensive updating should be actively considered. This work was to include repairs to the tower itself, more especially the hanging-frame and the bell-cap; re-casting and re-tuning the existing six bells plus the addition of two new bells. Thus Clun was to have a 'ring of eight', not common in a rural church. Large tenor bells can be several tons in overall weight, with smaller ones each weighing a few hundred pounds. They are usually cast in bronze and it is, of course, imperative that the tower structure and the metal bell-frames are of sufficient strength to support their musical associates. Testimony to the campanologists' skill, the eight bells of Clun could be rung through 40,320 changes, a feat which must have taken several hours.

Work to the bell-frame and the enlargement of the belfry was carried out by Day & Son of Suffolk. On 22ⁿᵈ July 1914 the bells were returned. They were collected from Broome Railway Station on two drays decorated with sweet-smelling flowers, laurels and yew branches. The procession was headed by the Rev H J Scott, followed by school teachers, Mr Short and Mrs Cleeton, and all the children, waving flags and carrying bunches of flowers or banners. The church organist and local clergy were succeeded by parish councillors, church-wardens and Trinity Almsmen.

The following extracts from the Shrewsbury Chronicle of 24ᵗʰ July and 25ᵗʰ September 1914 capture the mood:

"24 July. The church bells were welcomed back to Clun after being away to be re-cast and at the same time two more added to their number, making a total of eight. The clergy, choir, church officials, school children and a very large number of parishioners met the two drays, on which were carried the bells, outside the town and formed a long procession to the church gates. The town was decorated and banners and flags were carried in the procession which was preceded by the Rev. H. J. Scott. One banner bore the inscription '1668 Peace be unto Clun', which had been copied from one of the old bells."

"25 September. The dedication festival of the re-opening of the tower, dedication of the bells, the clock and the font cover was continued on Sunday last. The preacher at the 11 a.m. service was the Rev. C. W. O. Jenkin, Oxford and at Evensong, the Rev. A. E. Ll. Kenyon, Rector of Ludlow. Peels on the bells were rung during the day in which the Rev. V. A. Creswell and Messrs R. Marston JP and others took part."

Two decorated drays, complete with the new bells, pause at the bottom of the drive to The Hurst, having reached the boundary between Clunbury and Clun parishes.

The procession welcoming the bells crosses Clun Bridge and makes its way up Church Street. The Rev Harold Scott leads the entourage. The neatly-dressed children dutifully walking up the hill could not possibly be responsible for the mis-spelling of the first word on the banner! The former Temperance Hotel, built in 1870, and shown opposite the second banner, is now postcard dealer Pete Robards' Tea Shop that stocks examples of early postcards.

The bells arrive outside the church where the choir stand at the lych-gate entrance. (Two further bells were to be added in 1993.)

The new bells have been unloaded and stand displayed at the west door of the church. The dignitaries shown are from the left: Rev Vaughan (Newcastle on Clun), William Mead (Shopkeeper and Churchwarden), Rev Harold Scott (Curate), George Townsend (Farmer and Churchwarden), Rev Richard Machen (Vicar), William Darroll (Chemist and Churchwarden, John Davies (Parish Clerk), Unknown, Rev Gerald Cope (Curate).

The two new bells are pictured on the left and the one on the extreme left is inscribed: 'To the memory of Clara Creswell who died 17th July 1886'.

ENFIELD STREET   1928

The image shows Enfield Street looking south towards the Square as the visitor enters the town from Bishop's Castle. To the left with its low roof are the premises of watchmaker and insurance agent, Walter Bottomley; the Buffalo Hotel faces the camera in the distance; the landlord of this well-known hostelry at the time was Charles Henry Lewis. Rumour has it that Sir Walter Scott stayed here whilst writing *The Betrothed* and *The Talisman*, published jointly as *Tales of the Crusaders* in 1825. The Buffalo has been closed for several years and its future remains uncertain.

THE HURST   1912

This property on the eastern outskirts of Clun is a small country mansion of coursed limestone with a symmetrical twin-gabled frontage and central entrance porch. It features significant ridge stacks and a family crest – a spread eagle – incorporated within the roof parapet. Built for the Morris family circa 1813, it was the centre of a large country estate, long since dismembered by auction. This pleasing gentleman's residence once had extensive stabling and an attractive octagonal dovecote. At the time of the photograph Cuthbert Aubrey Morris-Field was the occupant; the property was later to become the home of John Osborne, author of *Look Back in Anger* fame. It is now run by the Arvon Foundation, which organises courses for writers, a fitting memorial to the late playwright.

CLUN SHOW   1922

The town band cross the river bridge in June 1922; they head a mock-up aeroplane and other decorative floats, a procession including dancers and a maypole troupe, and numerous other groups all participating in the jollifications. These include the Clun Comrades – a predecessor of the British Legion – the Ancient Order of Foresters, and the local Oddfellows. After parading around the town, they would all congregate on the castle grounds. The stonemason's yard to the right was that of John Roberts; his brother, William Roberts, had his timber yard adjacent. Clun Show continues to be held annually, usually in August.

CLUN'S 'OLD MARY'   1910

The photographer, Robert Newton Heyworth, left us with a puzzle when he chose this caption. Maybe he did not have wide distribution in mind when he stopped to ask if the sitter would care to pose for him. Maybe the title is indicative of deference towards the sweet old lady, protecting her privacy and evident advanced years. So who was Old Mary, and what was her age at the time of this photograph? Any information gratefully received!

THE UNVEILING OF THE WAR MEMORIAL   1921

The Union flag lies on the handrail to the entrance steps after the unveiling of the new War Memorial by the Bishop of Hereford on 5th June 1921. The grey Cornish stone remembrance cross was erected at a cost of £340 raised by public subscription. The plinth includes the names of 31 'Men of Clun' who gave their lives for their country in the First World War. The Bishop, the Right Rev William Lutener, and the Rev Harold Scott together with the choir lead the singing, while Clun's policeman, Thomas Crowe, stands to attention on the steps overseeing the large crowd of townsfolk. The rear of the postcard is of interest in that it was sent personally by Rev Scott to a Miss Bromley in Rhyl, North Wales.

TRINITY HOSPITAL ALMSMEN   1907

Our mutual friend Heyworth must have made a prior appointment with the warden, or how else would all these elderly gentlemen have been gathered together in one spot at a given time? There were usually 18 pensioners of limited means in residence. All wore the distinctive hat and gown; and at this time they received the sum of ten shillings per week. Heating and lighting were provided, as were most of their food needs, and they received free medical attention. In return, and according to their personal capabilities, they carried out menial tasks around the hospital and in the town. Unsurprisingly, there were many great characters among the almsmen, including Joe the Bear – John Weale, formerly of Newcastle on Clun, Billy Canty whose brother was the butcher at Clunton, – and Tommy 'Tappin' Williams, who had previously lived in Ford Street. The Trinity Hospital gates continue to be opened every morning, the public being welcome to visit.

THE MAY FAIR – THE MARKET PLACE   1906

A social history gem! A wonderful record of the 11th Annual May Fair with townsfolk and visitors starting to gather in the Market Square, all looking forward to meeting old friends and relatives, having fun and generally enjoying the day. Butcher Francis Griffiths hangs his meat prominently in his shop on the left; whilst behind the market stall the White Horse public house, run by Elizabeth Graves, awaits the expected rush of customers. A bearded policeman, with his white gloves tucked under his belt, keeps a watchful eye on the photographer, simultaneously diligently supervising the proceedings. At this time, part of the Town Hall/Old Market in the centre background was made available as a temporary gaol on Fair Days, no doubt for locking up miscreants, at least until such time as they had sobered up. Most of the streets would have market stalls set up, and Charlie Farrell's Grand Royal Racing Cocks merry-go-round from Chester would be just one of the many side shows, swing-boats, shooting galleries, coconut shies and boxing booths, all of which helped to make it a day to savour and later recall with affection. In 1909 the first moving pictures to come to Clun were shown at the May Fair.

1.2   *Chapel Lawn – Snugly Set Amongst the Hills*

THE SMITHY   1913

Unquestionably, another Heyworth prize image! A lady does not appear to be present in this wonderful all-action shot, but a lady it was who was in charge of this blacksmith's and farrier's in 1913. Mrs John Adams was the lady in question, and it is assumed that she had taken over from her husband, John, both in name and deed. He and his family had moved from Cleobury Mortimer in 1882 and his descendants continued in business at Chapel Lawn until the 1970s. During this time many local farmers repeatedly brought their working horses for re-shoeing, as did the sporting and society personalities of the area. There is no need to remind the true countryman of the importance of the hard-working farrier, and that all horses need their 'footwear' replaced periodically. This is a particularly well-composed picture, the icing on the cake being the way Heyworth has captured the sunlight filtering through the trees.

CAER CARADOC, CARACTACUS' CAMP   1922

This historic site lies three miles south-south-east of Clun. Dominating the Redlake Valley, this hill fort, an imposing earthwork, is a pear-shaped enclosure covering two hectares. Tradition has it that the Iron Age chieftain, Caractacus, fortified the site with a series of banks and ditches, and this is where he is said to have fought the Romans under Ostorius in AD 151. Custom also suggests that after his inevitable defeat by a much superior force, Caractacus was eventually taken to Rome where he was treated like a hero.

1.3 Newcastle on Clun – Offa's World

THE CROWN INN   1913

Situated four miles from Clun on the road to Anchor, Kerry and Newtown, the Crown hostelry in the small village of Newcastle on Clun is a popular stopping-off point for walkers on nearby Offa's Dyke, as it was for local artisans anxious to quench their thirst and bring themselves up-to-date with current village happenings. Built in the 17th century, the inn sits close to the confluence of the Folly Brook with the River Clun. Richard Jones was the landlord in 1913 when he was able to provide stabling for six horses.

1.4 Llanfair Waterdine/Skyborry – Upper Teme Haven

THE VILLAGE   1920

Absolute solitude in a small border village! The white house in the middle distance is The Hawthorns. Built in 1790, it was at one time the dame school where for a nominal charge of one old halfpenny per day each pupil was guaranteed to receive a good general education. In 1920 a Mr Edward Bright was the master in charge. The school was used in 1993 as the set for the film *Second Best* starring John Hurt. To the left is the old tithe barn, originally used for storing animal fodder, but at the time of the photograph its main use seems to be as parish bill-board. The building to the right was the Red Lion Inn, now renamed The Waterdine, constructed in 1570 as a Welsh longhouse, it was later used as a drovers' inn. The River Teme flows at the bottom of the garden of what is now a licensed restaurant and demarcates the boundary between England and Wales.

THE PARISH CHURCH OF ST MARY   1931

This edifice is considered to be a particularly 'good' example of wanton Victorian vandalism. Apparently, on this site there stood until 1853, a rare example of medieval ecclesiastical architecture, a church with carved oak pillars, an array of carved box pews and superb roof timbers. There is every probability that at that time the old building was in a poor state of repair, and there is known to have been much controversy locally as to which way to jump – to repair or replace. The decision was taken to replace old with new! Thomas Nicholson of Hereford was the architect of what is generally considered to be a rather plain church in coursed limestone rubble, sterile and uninteresting, with few redeeming features – its trussed rafter roof and re-crafted intricately carved communion rail are but two. The pine pews are nicely inscribed with the names of local farms within the parish. An unusual organ incorporates a barrel organ which can still play several tunes. In 1869 and 1870, a horse named The Colonel, bred by Mr Hamar of nearby Bicton and trained by John Davies of Cwmannum Farm, won the Grand National. After his last victory, The Colonel was led to St Mary's where a special service was held in his honour.

SKYBORRY   1919

On the minor road north-west from Knighton to Llanfair Waterdine, the traveller will first encounter the small hamlet of Nether Skyborry, followed almost immediately by its twin, Skyborry Green. The picture shows Skyborry Farm which is situated between the two hamlets. Situated 650 feet above sea-level and surrounded by lofty hills, these hamlets hug the northern banks of the Upper Teme Valley. This is superb walking country with scenery to match. Lord Hunt, leader of the successful 1953 Everest Expedition, lived at Skyborry for ten years after World War II.

Chapter Two

The Hundred of Purslow

Bedstone
Bishop's Castle
Bucknell
Clunbury
Clungunford
Clunton
Edgton
Hopesay
Hopton Castle
Lydbury North

2.1 Bedstone – Diminutive Hillside Parish

BEDSTONE CHURCH   1933

With its timber-framed 17th century bellcote and 19th century shingled broach spire, St Mary Magdalene is a small late-Norman church of coursed limestone rubble, placed in an elevated position on a hillside. Thereabouts, is a 17th century square-framed cottage and miniature schoolroom in a pseudo-Gothic style. Much repair work was carried out in 1851, but in 1879 architect F R Kempson of Hereford was entrusted with extensive restoration work at a cost of £1,200, yet further refurbishment taking place in 1903. The interior is gifted with a plain 12th century tub font, and the stained glass windows by Kempe are of high quality. There is seating for 90 parishioners. The register dates from 1719.

BEDSTONE COURT   1933

A large Victorian mansion in the so-called Old English style, Bedstone Court was designed by Thomas Harris for Sir Henry Ripley Bt, MP for Bradford, and completed in 1884 at a cost of £50,000. Harris was also the architect for Stokesay Court, built five years later. Ostensibly a calendar house, it reputedly has 12 chimneys, 365 windows, 52 rooms and 7 entrances. The Ripley family resided here until 1903 when the Langleys from Lancashire rented the property until 1940. During the war years it was used as a school for children evacuated from the south coast. In 1948, Mr R J Rees founded Bedstone Court School. A serious fire devastated the main building in 1996 but fortunately the principal rooms were not affected, and two years later all the damaged areas had been reinstated. It remains in educational use today.

2.2 Bishop's Castle – Chartered Borough

PARISH CHURCH OF ST JOHN THE BAPTIST   1919

The medieval parish church was largely rebuilt in 1860 and little of the original edifice survives. Placed at the lowest point of the town, its battlemented west tower, more especially the lower elements, is of the 15th century. Much damage was caused during the defeat of the Royalist forces in the Civil War and extensive restoration took place from 1648 onwards. A plain tub font of the late-Norman period survives. The tower accommodates six bells, and the register dates from 1559.

THE HIGH STREET   1926

Surprisingly, not a lot has changed in the intervening 80 years since this photograph was taken, the most obvious exception being the presence in the street of a solitary example of what was soon to become the ubiquitous motor car. The Town Hall with its clock dominates the scene at the top of the steadily rising High Street, whilst the Midland Bank to the right and its compatriot Barclays, a little higher up and jutting out onto the pavement, await their customers in those early days of banking. Parking is not a problem: the bull-nosed Morris, registration number UX 3233, has its front wheel turned into the kerb, the driver obviously not trusting such newfangled machinery. It must have been pleasant to chat across the highway without excessive traffic noise. The extensive post office building is just off camera to the right; it was here that postmaster, Alex Bore, headed a ten-strong workforce at the time. The weekly market was held on the ground floor of the Town Hall, and it was caretaker, Mrs Emma Kinsey, who was responsible for keeping this area and the first floor Council Chamber spick and span. One notable trader at the top of the rise was Edward C Davies at numbers 34 and 36; regrettably, this family ironmongery business closed in 2008 after a century of trading.

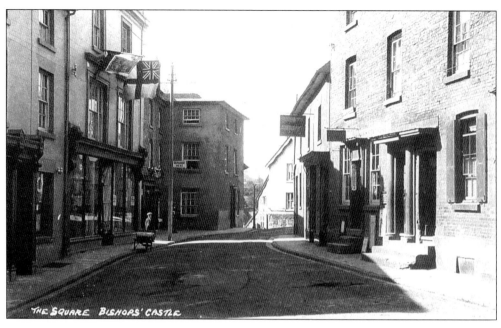

THE MARKET SQUARE   1926

A quiet day in this small market town! Bishop's Castle during the Middle Ages had been prosperous, but by the early 19th century its relative wealth had declined to that of a large village. The town, a 'rotten borough', held constituency status in its own right but was probably under the overall control of one, or perhaps two, wealthy landowners – its patron or patrons. The town would have had a low number of voters, for few people had the right to vote; furthermore, there was no secret ballot. Such conditions enabled candidates to buy their way to victory. Often two Members of Parliament were eligible for election by this highly unsatisfactory method. Needless to say such practices were eventually abolished with the passing of the 1832 Reform Act. The building in the sunlight at the far end of the Square is the Black Lion Inn, where Allen Davies was the landlord. In this part of the town were the premises of George Strawson, who with his daughter, Madge, operated a very successful photographic business until just after the First World War. He left a legacy of several hundred social and military history postcards, featuring not only the immediate area but further afield, well known to collectors and much sought after.

2.3 Bucknell – Expansive and Attractive

THE OLD MILL   1912

One of three mills located close to one another, all fed by the Redlake River, a tributary of the Clun, it was a corn grinding mill accepting cereal from local farmers, the end-product being used for both human consumption and animal feed. A weir dam provided water storage facilities in times of summer drought. Two out of the three mill buildings have survived and are now solely used for domestic purposes. This image is believed to show the mill known as Lower Mill, of which nothing remains, modern bungalows now occupying the site. Furthermore, no technical details regarding the mill's construction and machinery now exist.

THE RIVER BRIDGE   1916

The Redlake River passes under three bridges as it flows through Bucknell village. This particular bridge, built largely of rubble stonework, carries the main B4367 Craven Arms to Knighton road and consists of two 14-foot span arches made of brick. The old thatched cottage has long since been demolished, whilst the buildings in the centre are the Railway Tavern, with Sherwood's the butcher's premises behind. It was not until the 1920s that a piped water supply was provided from a well above Chapel Lawn. Before that time all water for household needs would have had to be carried from the Redlake River. This source was, therefore, vital to meet many demands, from providing water for animals to the cooling of machinery.

THE ELEMENTARY SCHOOL   1912

The very first school in Bucknell was established in the 17th century for those willing and able to pay the necessary attendance fees. The present St Mary's C of E School was built in 1865 on land given to the church for this purpose. Original documents state that the school was for those children whose parents were in straitened circumstances, in other words those who could not afford to pay a minimal amount per week. The headmaster appointed in 1867 was 24-year-old Mr Henry Evans. Mr Charles Lloyd was headmaster and Miss Jukes the assistant teacher at the time of this photograph. Coal fires or, at best, Tortoise stoves were then the only form of heating alongside oil lamps for lighting. All rather dismal in winter! Major extensions and updating took place in 1966, thus enabling meals to be cooked on the premises; additional classroom facilities were also provided.

PARISH CHURCH OF ST MARY   1908

Of likely 12th century foundation, the church was probably rebuilt in the 14th century. However, much of what you see is the result of extensive restoration work completed in 1870. St Mary's west gallery and pews were removed at this time and a new lean-to north aisle, organ chamber, south porch and vestry added. The 15th century nave roof of trusses with collar and tie beams was also restored, more particularly by the extensive renewal of the boarding. The west bell-tower was also rebuilt with its slated spirelet. All this work was carried out under the direction of Thomas Nicholson of Hereford. Nonetheless, the arch to the north wall of the chancel is of the 14th century, as is the blocked priest's doorway and undressed masonry in the nave. The bowl to the font is a noteworthy survivor of the early Norman period. The register dates from 1598.

THE MEMORIAL HALL   1924

As its name suggests, this building was erected in memory of servicemen who fell in World War I. Money was raised by fundraising events, and volunteers set about the building of this new hall for community use. For the sum of two shillings and sixpence anyone could add a brick to the foundations. The land was donated by the Sitwell family, and a military-type hut was purchased from Prees Heath Camp, North Shropshire. The village carpenter and undertaker, William Burgoyne, was the organising craftsman and he, along with many others, eventually completed the timber building. It was opened by the Member of Parliament for the area, Windsor Clive, in 1920. A plaque inside remembers the fallen of both world wars. The Memorial Hall has now served the community for almost 90 years and is in urgent need of replacement by a modern, purpose-built structure. To this end, there is presently a scheme in hand to raise the necessary funds and obtain grant aid.

STATION ROAD   1909

On the right, partly hidden by foliage, the Sitwell Arms was presided over by landlady Mrs Elizabeth Powell, whose daughter stands outside the pub looking at the cameraman. At this time, there was stabling available for 20 horses. Meanwhile, the local postman, Arthur Whittle, approaches with a cartload of coal for delivery to customers around the village. He apparently needed to indulge in a bit of 'moonlighting'! The public house is named after a branch of the Derbyshire Sitwell family who lived at Ferney Hall, between Onibury and Clungunford. William H Hurt-Sitwell, who was Lord of the Manor and a principal landowner, lived at The Cottage in Bucknell for a number of years. The Clun Forest Sheep Society, an organisation of worldwide influence, was inaugurated at the Sitwell Arms in 1925.

9

TYPE.

CLUN FOREST SHEEP BREEDERS' SOCIETY.

A Definition of the Characteristics of a Clun Forest Sheep, as adopted at the Annual General Meeting of Members held on January 27th, 1928.

STANDARD.

HEAD AND FACE.—A clean open dark-brown face, free from speckles, top of head nicely covered and free from dark wool.

EARS.—Not too long. Free from speckles and carried high.

BODY.—Strong muscular neck, lengthy good back, deep rib, strong loin, good dock, deep and well rounded thighs, good through heart, strong bone, standing square on its legs.

LEGS.—Free from speckles, fairly free from wool from hock and knee down.

WOOL.—A tight fleece, fine texture, free from kemp and dark or grey wool.

SKIN.—A nice pink or red skin, free from black or blue spots.

A Sheep which meets you with a good head and a bold walk, that stands squarely on its legs, with plenty of heart girth and a good constitution.

THE RAILWAY STATION   1920

Situated on the Heart of Wales line from Craven Arms to Swansea, which somehow survived the Beeching axe of the 1960s, Bucknell station, though unfinished, was opened in October 1860 and 100 years ago was a very busy place. The day started when Bucknell newsagent, Bill Shaw, met the early mail train with his handcart and picked up the daily papers. Ten staff were required to service the various station facilities, and they were responsible for the loading and unloading of all goods, including animal feedstuffs, farm machinery, furniture, milk churns, parcels, in fact every known domestic requirement. In those days everything was moved by train. Up to 30 mailbags are known to have been handled each working day. Timber from Davies' yard, adjacent to the railway station, was loaded and sent to destinations nationwide. Additionally, up to 15 wagons of coal per day were shunted into the goods yard, mostly from the East Shropshire and Wyre Forest Coalfields. The horse and cart was still the principal method of delivery to local customers. The photograph shows a London and North Western Railway coal tank on a passenger service; prospective passengers await the arrival of the train together with attentive and expectant staff.

THE VILLAGE POST OFFICE   1909

Another delightful pastoral image! As in many other villages, the location of the post office changed rather frequently during the late 19th and early 20th centuries; invariably, however, it was in the residence of the sub-postmaster or postmistress. Bucknell was no different, and here it was situated in a picturesque thatched cottage alongside the Redlake River. The post office, together with the integral village shop, was run by the Sherwood and Picken families for at least 30 years from 1900. The Bucknell premises were an important communications link in the border counties; apart from housing the embryonic telegraph facilities, the post office employed eight postmen and required two vans to service a widely scattered area of some 20 square miles.

BUCKNELL TURNPIKE – TEME VALLEY HOUNDS   1908

This image is of the old Bucknell Turnpike on the Knighton to Brampton Bryan road near Lingen Bridge and the turn-off to Bucknell. The picture is full of interest: the ladies on the left have arrived in their Sunday best, some on bicycles, whilst gentry in pony and traps watch the proceedings intently from the rear. Meanwhile, a rival photographer has just arrived and hurries to set up his equipment behind the horses. The rider in the bowler hat, centre stage, is Geoff Harley of Brampton Bryan Hall, and to the right is Sir Henry Ripley of Bedstone Court.

2.4 Clunbury – Quaint and Quiet

THE PARISH CHURCH OF ST SWITHIN   1906

One of Robert Newton Heyworth's earliest postcards, published soon after his arrival in Knighton. This beautifully positioned church, placed high overlooking the village, was built during the 12th century and was originally a chapel of ease to its mother church at nearby Clun, itself attaining parochial status in 1341. The solid-looking west tower is of the latter date, though 17th century above corbel height. The south doorway is late Norman, and a new west door was added in 1842. Victorian restoration came in 1881 when Birrell's of Shrewsbury carried out the work including the addition of a new entrance porch, all at a cost of £1,654. The tower, strengthened in the late 1940s, holds six bells, the oldest dated 1620; two are of 1631, and the last three were added in 1887 to commemorate Queen Victoria's Golden Jubilee. The tower clock was installed in 1900. There are seats for 250 parishioners, and the register dates from 1574.

A VILLAGE SCENE   1912

A view of the village street in Clunbury looking south towards Clunbury Hill. A small, compact settlement just off the main route from Craven Arms to Clun, Clunbury sits snugly in the river valley between the main road and rising ground to the south. Life locally has changed more than a smidgen since the all-providing Edwardian era when residents could satisfy virtually every need on their own doorsteps. The villager now has to go further afield for all the usual services, except of course that provided by the church. It was a descendant of William Cooper, one-time farrier here, who was to make a fortune out of Australian sheep farmers with his Cooper's Sheep-Dip, a proven remedy for the prevention of ticks on woolly herbivores. The timber-framed, black-and-white cottage to the right housed the sub-post office in the period just before the First World War, and it was here that Frederick Mold dispensed money orders and exchanged local gossip.

THE VILLAGE SCHOOL   1908

The camera has caught the children during playtime, and the headmaster, Mr W E Deacon, is just visible in the doorway. The school was opened in July 1862 to cater for 110 pupils, the land being purchased on behalf of the church by the then vicar, the Rev William Jellicourse, a reverend gentleman who looked after his flock for over 40 years from 1856. The aforementioned Mr William Edwin Deacon was headmaster from 8th October 1877 until his retirement on 5th September 1918. His reputation was as a man of strict discipline, able to achieve high educational standards from his pupils. His wife, Louisa, was infant teacher for much of this time. His successor was Mr Joe Cooper, who remained the school's headmaster until 1950. There must have been something in the water!

THE ODDFELLOWS WALK   1907

With their large banner gusting in the wind, members of the Vale of Clun Lodge of Oddfellows (a Benevolent or Friendly Society) are shown marching to their meeting place at nearby Purslow. The Clunbury Oddfellows Branch was formed in 1888 and was affiliated to the Manchester Unity. Membership was open to all, and there were no political or religious affiliations. However, some branches were confined to the working classes only. Sports, fetes and other fundraising events were held throughout the Clun Valley, essentially to support members in need.

THE ODDFELLOWS WALK   1907

Children stand obediently at the roadside looking neat and tidy in their pinafore dresses and straw hats as the Oddfellows pass by. The men all wear their identifying sashes, together with either cloth cap or bowler. What was the distinction? Mr Deacon, the headmaster of Clunbury School, was a founder member of his local lodge and became its hard-working secretary in 1909. Presumably the children would cheerfully join the rear of the parade, anticipating the tea and cakes that were to follow the procession!

THE HUNDRED HOUSE, PURSLOW   1907

This hostelry, situated on the B4368 between Aston on Clun and Clunton, was built in 1685, probably on the site of an earlier building. James Warish was the licensee here at the time of the photograph, when facilities included stabling for 12 horses. The premises were owned by the Earl of Powis; he was later to lease and eventually sell the property to the People's Refreshment House Association in 1926. The inn's title is derived from the Anglo-Saxon division of the county into Hundreds, of which Purslow was one of 15 in Shropshire.

PURSLOW HALL BAZAAR   1907

Purslow is a manor house of the early 17th century, possibly 1628, with later additions. Of red brick with slate roofs, this large property was originally built to an 'H' plan; internally some of the ground-floor rooms include original panelling. The photograph shows the pierrots preparing to give their display on the rear lawn, watched by an expectant audience. The bazaar was held to raise money for the Clunbury Nursing Association, of which Mrs Harriet Heber-Percy of Purslow Hall was treasurer. The funds raised at this and other events were used to fund the annual salary of a district nurse and for the provision of a bicycle to enable her to discharge her duties in the area.

LITTLE BRAMPTON, WHEELWRIGHT'S SHOP   1909

Situated in Clunbury parish on the main road between Aston on Clun and Purslow, this image shows the wheelwright, John Lewis, standing by the gate with his wife, Kate, directly behind him in the doorway. John came from nearby Bedstone and his wife from Hopesay, and they had three children: Charles, Kathleen and Roland. Also included in the picture are wheelwrights Charles Jones of Clunbury, Harry Morris of Uffington, Caleb Langford from Leintwardine, and carpenter George Lloyd. A stack of wheel hubs lie to the left of the shed, ready for use. This long-established wheelwright's shop served the district for many years, until Tom Perkins changed its usage to a builder's yard. It is now a popular tea room.

Telephone : LITTLE BRAMPTON 1   ESTIMATES FREE

JOHN LEWIS & SON

Builders, Plumbers and Undertakers

LITTLE BRAMPTON
CRAVEN ARMS, SALOP

2.5 Clungunford – Gunnas to the Natives

CLUNGUNFORD.CHURCH (98.A)

ST CUTHBERT'S PARISH CHURCH   1912

St Cuthbert's was built early in the 14th century under the patronage of the Fitzalans, Earls of Arundel and Lords of Clun, although the north aisle is possibly a little earlier. The walls are of buff-coloured local rubble stone. It is a spacious building, light and imposing. Nothing changed here for nearly 500 years. But the restoration of St Cuthbert's in the mid-1890s by architect Edward Turner of Leicester was significant and comprehensive, including a new south porch, new north tower, alterations to windows, and general titivation to all things internal. The overall cost was said to be £2,530, mostly paid for by the then Lord of the Manor, Mr J L C Rocke of Clungunford House. The oldest bell is dated 1350, and their numbers have steadily increased until in 1997 the sixth and final bell was installed. The register dates from 1574.

CHANCEL CLYNGUNFORD CHURCH

PARISH CHURCH, INTERIOR   1912

This image perfectly illustrates the chancel of St Cuthbert's. The 1895 restoration work is much in evidence, including the £758 new organ built by James Binns of Leeds. The font is of Wenlock limestone and dated 1835. The two stained-glass windows are Victorian, by John Hardman.

THE RECTORY 1913

This fine, imposing Victorian rectory replaced an earlier inadequate timber-framed building. Of brick, multi-gabled and with patterned roof tiles as well as both mullion and transom stone details to windows, the property cost £1,267 to build in 1858, the architect responsible being A E Perkins of Worcester. Four members of the local Rocke family were rectors here between 1779 and 1945. Apparently not entirely congenial as far as later incumbents were concerned, it was perhaps rather cold and draughty, so much so that circa 1970 the rectory was sold and converted to flats.

CLUNGUNFORD HOUSE 1912

Trees partially obscure the splendour of Clungunford House, the home of the Rocke family; it was built in 1828 to a design by Edward Haycock of Shrewsbury for the Rev John Rocke. The frontage is of red brick, but other elevations have been rendered. This neat two-storied house with Tuscan/Doric columns to the front entrance porch has an interior which is vaguely Grecian in style, with an elegant grand central staircase. John Rocke 1817-81 was renowned for his rare collection of stuffed birds which included an extinct "Great Auk", best described as an Icelandic mini penguin. He purchased the Great Auk in 1860 and it remained in his collection until well after his death. It was sold in 1936 for £700 and again in 1971 for £9000. What would it be worth to-day? It is presently on display at the Birmingham museum. The last of the Rocke squires, John, died in 1985. He was a well-respected gentleman who was High Sheriff of Shropshire and represented his area on the County Council. The estate of several hundred acres was broken up and sold by auction.

THE SCHOOL   1910

As in many other villages, education in Clungunford was originally provided by the church, the diocesan authorities having overall authority, and local lords of the manor providing financial support. At the end of the 18th century lessons were being held in the church itself. In 1857, John Rocke of Clungunford House donated half an acre of land on which to erect a purpose-built school, and work started immediately on a Victorian Gothic style building with adjacent school-house. The materials used were brick for the internal walls, the external walls being of local limestone. The total cost was £726. Accommodation was provided for 90 pupils, and Mr William Holland was the first master to be appointed. In 1948 the school roll at Clungunford was affected by legislation raising the school leaving age to 15, with children over 11 being sent to a local secondary school, either to Craven Arms, Bishop's Castle or Ludlow. The village school closed on 26th July 1961, the property being sold 12 years later, and it is now a private residence.

BROADWARD HALL   1910

In the parish of Clungunford and once part of the Hopton Castle Estate, Broadward Hall stands near the 'broad ford' over the River Clun, from which its name is derived. With its Regency Gothic battlements, this 18th century house has the appearance of a small castle. The Bayley family lived here for 200 years. Subsequent owners included Bilston Corporation which purchased the property in 1943 for conversion to a children's home, but this venture came to nothing. In 1947 Thomas Watkins became the new owner, and farmed the 124-acre estate. It is now a country house of some character owned by the Skyrme family.

FERNEY HALL 1912

There is every possibility that there was a 16th century building on this site, but Ferney Hall, situated two miles south-west of Onibury, has certainly had a chequered history. In 1858 John Norton was commissioned by the Sitwells to design a country residence, but that structure is unrecognisable today, for it was completely rebuilt by the Shrewsbury architect, S Pountney Smith, some 20 years later following a disastrous fire. Although symmetrical in design, the over-fussy neo-Jacobean style did not receive many plaudits. The extravagant three-storey house fell into disrepair between the wars, and was finally abandoned in 1952. However, although the property was in an advanced state of decay, it was reprieved in 2002; major restoration was undertaken, and works completed in 2006.

ABCOTT MANOR 1919

Clungunford's Abcott Manor is not a manor in the true sense, for it was not the home of a medieval lord, but a 17th century country gentleman's dwelling. Timber-framing, mainly vertically panelled, is complemented internally by moulded ceilings and wood panelling. This attractive residence replaced an earlier house, probably dating from the 13th century. The Morris family lived here for over a century; the heiress, Beatrice Morris, married Wrottesley Prynce, a wealthy grandson of the Shrewsbury Royalist, Sir Richard Prince, who was Mayor of Shrewsbury in 1662 and was responsible for building Whitehall, a sandstone town residence in Monkmoor Road. Their descendants continued to own Abcott until the early 1800s, when the property and its 355 acres passed to the Rocke family's Clungunford Estate. The holding was sold off in separate lots in the 1980s, and Abcott is now a private residence.

2.6 Clunton – Hill Fort Country

BURY DITCHES   1912

Difficult to photograph successfully, except from the air, Bury Ditches lies two miles north of Clunton. This exceptional hill fort stands nearly 1200 feet above sea-level on Summerhill summit and covers an area of four hectares. Elliptical in shape, its massive earthworks include defensive ramparts, more especially to the north side; the two long and steep passage entrances are very impressive, and all date from 500BC. For its time, it was a major engineering feat!

FOOTBRIDGE AND FORD   1910

Yet another nostalgic scene captured by Heyworth! Just south of the Crown Inn, this old footbridge consisted of stone piers and intermediate timber supports. In the 1920s it was noticed by a Mr E Jervoise, traveller and author, who recognised it as being of some antiquity. At that time, some work had recently been done to its timber deck and handrails, but the knowledgeable traveller was sufficiently taken by what he described as 'a very old bridge', that he included details in his work *Ancient Bridges of Wales and Western England*. A concrete bridge erected in the 1960s now crosses this spot, no trace remaining of the demolished footbridge. The same fate befell the adjacent old cottage of Beattie Thomas and Bert Evans – this property, because of its proximity to the Clun, was regularly subject to flooding. This rural scene is no more, so this image is valuable archive material.

THE CROWN INN   1922

Clunton residents could quench their thirst at one of two pubs in the first quarter of the 20th century. The Crown Inn is the sole survivor. John Jones was the landlord in the 1920s, and there is every possibility that it is his wife who stands in the doorway; there was once stabling for six horses. It is known that a beer-house existed on the site in the 17th century. As with many other country inns, its survival has been in doubt, but in 1994 a consortium of villagers purchased the licensed premises, and the pub remains open for custom to this day.

THE MILL   1910

This early 19th century stone-built corn mill had an internal undershot wheel of 16-foot diameter and 5-foot width, with a 16-inch axle. The arms and paddles were of wood, bosses and rims of iron. Its horizontal lay shaft system, without upright shaft, drove two pairs of grindstones. A chain-driven pulley operated the sack hoist in the loft; another large pulley operated the drive to the flour dresser. The mill had a 150-yard leat from the River Clun, with a relatively short tailrace. The miller at this time was Charles Jones, who was also landlord of the Crown Inn. The mill worked commercially until 1936. The timber-framed mill house with brick infill, formerly a farmhouse, is of the mid-17th century and has a massive, stepped external end stack. The house is now fully restored; the mill is undergoing restoration.

ST MARY'S PARISH CHURCH 1908

St Mary's, close beside the main road, was built in 1871 on the site of a medieval chapel; the architect on behalf of the diocesan authorities was Thomas Nicholson. Built as a chapel of ease to nearby St Swithin's at Clunbury, the small edifice was consecrated by the Bishop of Hereford on 2nd April 1871. Of local stone, it has a small nave and chancel in one, a north porch, ogee-cusped lancets, and a squat west bell turret. The ladies in their Sunday best face the camera, as do two of the local lads. One would be well advised not to linger on this busy road today.

THE VILLAGE SCHOOL 1913

It is playtime at Clunton School. The children pose, the girls in their white smocks, and the boys wearing their caps; some children play a formal game within a circle. This Church of England Infant School was built in 1878 to cater for 35 pupils, its first teacher being Miss M Beetham. The average number of pupils attending during the early 20th century was only 22, and the school closed in the 1930s. After years of neglect and a distinct lack of tender loving care, the premises were eventually refurbished and reopened as the village hall on 11th July 1998. Such usage continues today.

PRIMITIVE METHODIST CHAPEL   1908

Non-conformism had many followers in the Clun Valley in the 18th and 19th centuries, when services were always well attended. At first meetings were held in private houses, but in Clunton a local resident, Edward Williams, provided land for a new chapel. The building, as shown, cost £300 and was opened for worship in March 1871. In 1971 the building became a spice factory and since 1995 has been a private residence.

RIVER BRIDGE AND POST OFFICE   1906

Mrs Sarah Bloor was sub-postmistress at the post office situated to the right of the photograph, Heyworth having his back to the Crown Inn. Apart from Sarah's pre-occupation with all things postal, she also ran the premises as the village stores, and advertised that she had a threshing machine for hire. The main Clun to Craven Arms road crosses the Gunridge Brook Bridge; the road in the foreground heads for Clunton Coppice, with the Bury Ditches road disappearing into the distance. Clunton Coppice is surviving oak woodland, habitat of deer, and home to rare flora and the extremely uncommon fungus, Phillensus Robustus, which, rather unusually, grows on the high branches of the oaks. Incidentally, this area is an acknowledged walker's paradise.

STEPPLE FARM 1922

Stepple Farm nestles at the foot of Stepple Knoll, close to Bury Ditches and just a short distance north-west of Clunton village. The derivation of Stepple suggests 'a settlement in a steep place'. John Collins was farming here in 1922, and Gilbert Jones with his son have farmed it for the past 30 years. The area has always been regarded as good hunting territory by the local gentry; Stepple Farm is surrounded by steeply undulating, wooded hills, punctuated by watercourses. In medieval times Clunton had 'five hayes' – a haye being a fenced or hedged enclosure for holding deer – which serves to emphasise the importance of hunting to the Clunton area in the past.

THE ROYAL OAK 1909

It is probably George Milward, the landlord, standing in the doorway in this posed picture; on the other hand, it could be a footman keeping an eye on the horse and small landau whilst imbibing a quick glass of liquid refreshment. The Royal Oak closed its doors to drinkers in the early 1920s and is now a private residence.

CWM HALL   1910

The well-established South Shropshire Edwards family significantly changed 17th century Cwm Hall in 1863 by adding a new wing to the rear plus a lean-to porch, and making internal alterations. The oldest section of the property is timber-framed on a hewn masonry base, a distinctive feature being the massive stone-shouldered chimney stack. The mid-Victorian work was completed two years after the coming of the railway, and the owners provided a suitable carriageway covering the three or so miles from Cwm to Hopton Heath railway station to maximise the benefits of this new and faster means of transport. Where the public highway was non-existent, or to follow it would have meant a considerable detour, new hard-surfaced trackways were laid over estate-owned land. The Edwards family holding covered several thousand acres and remained intact until 1919, when it was sold off piecemeal.

Peter Todd, the founder in 1859 of the Victoria Mill, Wheelton, Chorley, Lancashire, became the new owner of the property at the turn of the century. Mr Todd continued updating and expanding his business enterprise and in 1892 had 1,092 steam-driven looms in operation, providing employment for many Chorley people, plus, of course, a profitable return for himself. Cwm Hall is tucked away to the north-east and within the lower folds of Black Hill (440 m). The author Bruce Chatwin wrote one of his novels, appropriately titled *On the Black Hill*, whilst staying at Cwm Hall in 1980.

THE FARM, CLUNTON   1908

Five timber-framed buildings lie within Clunton village, and this charming portrait of Old Farm is perhaps the best example. The picturesque property dates back to the late 16th century, is now Grade II listed, and would originally have had a thatched roof. Price Goodwin and his son were overseeing operations here at the time of the photograph.

2.7 Edgton – Rural Solitude

VILLAGE SCENE   1925

Edgton, a small parish situated to the north of Hopesay and east of Lydbury North, is located in secluded and rather remote country on the southern extremities of the Long Mynd. The derivation of its name suggests 'home on the edge of a hill'. Humphrey Sandford of The Isle, Bicton, near Shrewsbury was the absentee lord of the manor a century ago. This scattered community of some 200 villagers could then boast a sub-post office, village shop, a boot and shoe repairer, butcher, wheelwright, blacksmith, an elementary school and a parish church. It could even cater for thirsty farmhands with a local beer-house, The Gate Hangs Well, which had stabling for four horses. The church survives, but not the other services. The thriving village hall is now the centre of an active community which is more than content with its peaceful isolation. An annual well-dressing ceremony is still practised here.

2.8 Hopesay – Sylvan Splendour

HOPESAY RECTORY AND CHURCH   1915

The rectory must have been very difficult to keep warm in the days of coal fires. A rambling property of many windows including dormers, possibly Victorian additions, it was far from the usual nicely proportioned Georgian residence. The living here once included 62 acres of glebe and was gifted by the Earl of Powis, Lord of the Manor. In more recent times, the building served as a high-class licensed guest house, but has lately reverted to a private residence.

HOPESAY, ST MARY – INTERIOR   1911

The interior of the parish church has changed little in the intervening years. The most obvious variation has been the replacement of the quaint hanging oil lamps with something a little more effective. Flowers decorate the window sills, a practice which continues to this day. The oak pulpit to the left was presented in 1897 in memory of General Green, and the double-chamfered chancel arch, centrepiece of the photograph, was rebuilt in the same year, but is undeniably 12th century in character. The stained-glass chancel window dates from 1858, a memorial to Capt Henry Beddoes RN, who died on 13th June 1856. The brass eagle lectern was presented to the parish by the parishioners of St John's, Drury Lane, London.

HOPESAY, ST MARY   1911

Attractively situated, but rather hidden away in a wooded valley, the parish church of St Mary with its distinctive broad and low west tower is basically a 12th century structure. The usual Victorian restoration took place, but the chancel, nave and tower are all of the early period and many other early features survive. The oak lych-gate is of 1892, its erection being paid for by the Rev R G Maul, in memory of his parents. The large parish includes Aston on Clun, Broome and Rowton. Personal memories of the author's association with the church remain strong; his daughter, Charlotte, sang in the choir here during her formative years.

HOPESAY, OAKFIELD   1912

Mr Heyworth got his caption wrong here: Oakfield is not in Aston on Clun – an irrefutable fact, for the house was the author's family home for 27 years until 2005! Soon after this photograph was taken Oakfield was renamed Hopesay House. Originally built by the Hopesay Estate with a coach house and stables nextdoor, this rather grand residence was adjacent to the Home Farm which had several hundred acres of pasture land. In its heyday the house was quite grand, having its own ballroom as well as 20 reception and bedrooms. Greatly reduced in size in 1956, it is now a much more manageable house of five bedrooms together with five acres of land. W A East resided here for many years, and it was during his long stay that he donated neighbouring Hopesay Hill and Common to the National Trust. Wooded Burrow Hill to the west has an early example of an Iron Age Fort at its summit, reputed to date from 100BC.

ASTON ON CLUN, ASTON HALL   1915

The Radnorshire and West Herefordshire Hunt appear ready to move off from the front drive of Aston Hall, having partaken of the traditional stirrup cup. Standing to the west of the village, the property was erected in 1837; Georgian in style, the 15-bedroomed country residence has a Greek/Doric columned entrance porch. Mr E J Artindale was in occupation in the years leading up to and including the First World War. He was followed by the Rev Sidney Dugdale who was resident here for much of the 1920s and '30s. During the Second World War, the property was used as offices by the Government Forestry Agency and was sold by the Oaker Estate in 1949. The building has recently been renovated and divided into apartments.

ASTON ON CLUN, MARRIAGE CELEBRATIONS   1906

The 18th April 1906 was a memorable day both in San Francisco and in the quiet rural community of Aston on Clun, both events being completely unrelated. Firstly, a severe earthquake, the initial shock lasting one minute, occurred in San Francisco, killing 3,000 people and injuring another 225,000.   Secondly, on the same day in a much more tranquil setting, Aston on Clun celebrated the wedding of the Rev William Charles Rocke, rector of nearby Clungunford, to Charlotte Mabel Artindale, daughter of E J Artindale of Aston Hall. The ceremony took place at Clungunford, a parish which the Rev Rocke was eventually to serve for 53 years. The photograph shows the magnificent welcoming arch erected over the Clun to Craven Arms Road outside the Kangaroo Inn. Its message reads: *As happy as the bridal morn may the evening of your life be*. It is not difficult to imagine the villagers all dressed up for the occasion and looking forward to the wedding tea on the lawns of Aston Hall.

ASTON ON CLUN, ROSE COTTAGES   1910

This postcard shows 1, 2 and 3 Rose Cottages, opposite the Kangaroo Inn. The property on the extreme right was the toll-gate cottage until the 1870s. Records show that Ann Davies was the toll-keeper here in 1851. One of the village pumps was situated in front of the cottages, and there was a cobbler's shed at the bottom of the garden.

ASTON ON CLUN, THE ARBOR TREE 1928

Situated in the centre of the village, this 300-year-old black poplar and its predecessors were decorated with flags annually on the Sunday nearest to 29th May. The custom is believed to be linked to the Celtic Princess, St Brigit, a goddess of fertility, and was perpetuated by Charles II, who by way of celebrating the restoration of the monarchy in 1660, proclaimed 29th May as Oak Apple Day and a national holiday. It is believed that the tree was decorated for the marriage of Richard Marston of Oaker and Mary Carter of nearby Sibdon in 1786, and the couple later made an annual donation to enable the tradition to continue. Unfortunately, in September 1995, the old tree blew down in a gale but was replaced with a sapling taken from the original just three months later. The image captures the doctor waiting for the arrival of the bus from Clun; he peers out from behind the trunk of the Arbor Tree, his essential black bag next to the lamp post.

ASTON ON CLUN, FORESTERS' MEETING 1911

The Ancient Order of Foresters, whose prime objective was to organise fundraising events, congregate outside the Kangaroo Inn. Here, as always, they are smartly turned-out: everyone has a collar and tie, and there are hats of every description, from straw boaters and bowlers to the working man's trademark cloth cap. The splendid embroidered silk banner was an important symbol of the organisation, and would be hoisted proudly at the head of their marches, which usually included stopping at the homes of local dignitaries where refreshments would be provided. The Round House, in the background, was formerly the village post office, where the carpenter Thomas Deakin was also the postmaster.

ASTON ON CLUN, OAKER   1910

Very much altered, Oaker is an early 17th century former farmhouse, its timber frame having been covered with roughcast rendering. Now a six-bedroomed gentleman's residence, it overlooks the River Clun and was originally known as Aston Mill Farm. For many generations it was the home of the Marston family, and it was not until 1949 that the house and its extensive holding of 937 acres was split up and sold at auction in various lots. Much of Hopesay, Beambridge, Broome and Aston on Clun were affected by the sale. The property had previously been sold in 1858 for the princely sum of £6,246, which included just 184 acres of land; in 2007, the house was again available for purchase, with just 20 acres of land, the asking price being £850,000!

ASTON ON CLUN, OAKER WEIR AND MILL   1910

Oaker Weir and Mill now lie in ruins to the rear of a timber-framed cottage adjacent to Oaker farmhouse. Overgrown with vegetation for many years, access is difficult. No machinery remains, although the penstock (floodgate/trough) was identifiable until recently. It was essentially an estate mill, grinding cereals for the landowner and his many tenants, both for human and animal consumption. Water from the one-mile leat from the River Kemp worked the undershot wheel, its tailrace flowing back into the River Clun. This arrangement involving the waters of two rivers may be unique! In the 1920s, when the corn mill became redundant, machinery was installed by the owner to generate electricity for properties in the immediate vicinity – Oaker itself, the farmhouse and farm cottages. Generation continued until 1940.

ASTON ON CLUN, THE BLACKSMITH'S SHOP AND ROUND HOUSE   1909

William Jones was the anvil man when this photograph was taken. The artisans captured by Mr Heyworth's lens were, from left to right: Fred Cadwallader, worker blacksmith, William Jones, owner, his son Edward and another son Maurice, whilst just visible to the left of the Round House are Thomas Deakin, wheelwright, and his domestic, Mary Hudson from the Round House. The identity of the young mother holding the baby is not known. Edward was to become the tenant after his father, and in 1949 purchased the adjoining Kangaroo Inn from the Oaker Estate for £5,400.

ASTON ON CLUN, THE ROUND HOUSE AND KANGAROO INN   1934

The petrol filling station run by local smallholder, John Humphreys, who lived at the Round House, has now moved ten yards to the old blacksmiths shop next to the Kangaroo. The Round House is of the Georgian period, circa 1780, built as an estate house and later used as the local post office. In the 1930s Cecil Edwin Purser was landlord of The Kangaroo, which in earlier pre-motor car days had stabling for 10 horses.

BROOME RAILWAY STATION   1925

This image shows the station approach when it was never busier! Built for the Knighton Railway, the station opened in the 1860's. Here, a large crowd of passengers make their way across the forecourt. They are members of the Mormon sect, who, together with many others, were congregating for their annual meeting held in a large marquee at Rowton Grange, about a mile south-east of Broome Station. These followers of the Church of the Latter Day Saints would have travelled here from all parts of the country.

BROOME STATION-MASTER'S HOUSE   1913

This substantially built station-master's house is strategically placed next to the station yard. The important incumbent would not miss much, even when he wasn't on duty! The house is of ashlar blocks with a slate roof and was completed in 1861 for the Knighton Railway. The goods yard at this time was a busy place, even considering its rural locality, with stabling for 16 horses. It was also home to Samuel and John Chester, Coal Merchants of Craven Arms. These two gentlemen were the author's great-great-grandfather and great-grandfather respectively.

'EXPRESS' COMING THROUGH BROOME STATION

BROOME STATION – A PASSING EXPRESS   1908

This is an evocative shot of a south-bound London and North Western express passing through Broome, the first station after Craven Arms, and the Shrewsbury to Hereford main line. Surprisingly, the train appears to be hauled either by a Webb 0-6-2 Coal Tank or a Webb 2-6-2 tank engine, both inappropriate motive power for express work. All this suggests that the railway company did not put this line anywhere near the top of its priority list.

With many level-crossings and speed restrictions, the line is not the fastest but passes through breathtaking scenery on its journey from the Shropshire Hills to Swansea Bay. It has to be remembered that in Victorian and Edwardian times, the railway was a lifeline, roads were non-existent or of a poor standard. Furthermore, the difficult terrain ensured that there was no opposition from navigable waterways. The railway was the workhorse, speedily conveying the mineral wealth of south and west Wales northwards to the industrial areas of the Midlands, Lancashire and Yorkshire. The remoteness of the line meant passenger numbers were low, the result being that the Heart of Wales Line was absolutely reliant on the movement of freight and the profit that generated. All of this traffic had to pass through Broome, a small country station, and in the days of steam the route could get very busy.

BROOME, THE TERRACE   1912

These four cottages were built for the London and North Western Railway Company in the 1880s to accommodate employees at the nearby railway station. They are situated opposite the station-master's house. William Owen, a signalman at Broome from 1897 until 1939, lived at No 4 for 33 years. These properties have recently been renovated and sold on the open market.

2.9 Hopton Castle – Civil War Siege

THE CASTLE RUINS   1912

This scheduled ruin, of which only the sandstone keep survives, was said to have been built in the reign of King Stephen (1135-54), but a later early-14th century date has recently been suggested as being more probable. Originally belonging to the De Say family, it passed to Osbert de Hopton in the mid-12th century. The Corbets were the owners three centuries later, before selling the castle to the Wallop family. In 1643, during the Civil War, Parliamentarian Henry Wallop installed 31 men under Colonel Samuel More to defend the castle against the Royalist Cavaliers. A year later the Cavaliers, under the command of Sir Michael Woodhouse, laid siege to the castle with 500 men, but failed to take it. An agreement was reached between the leaders; the fortress was to be surrendered in exchange for free passage. The result was the inevitable bloodbath, with only four Roundheads surviving the brutal betrayal, and Colonel More finding himself incarcerated within the walls of Ludlow Castle. It was Brampton Bryan's turn next!

ST EDWARD'S PARISH CHURCH   1912

Standing a little detached from its flock, St Edward's replaced the medieval church of St Mary, which was originally a chapel of ease to Clun, but a separate entity from 1291. St Mary's was demolished in the late 1860s. The rather plain Victorian replacement, designed by Hereford-based architect Thomas Nicholson, was built in 1870 in a vaguely neo-English Gothic style at a cost of £1,000. The church is of grey coursed rubble, ashlar-faced internally, comprising an undivided nave and chancel, south porch and vestry, with a western bell-turret housing two bells. Attractive stained glass installed in 1871 by Barnett of Newcastle is in memory of George Dansey Pardoe, rector for 45 years. The church holds very special memories for the author and his wife, Beryl, who were married at St Edward's in 1966.

THE RECTORY   1913

In a pretty village of numerous 17th century timber-framed cottages, it comes as no surprise to find that the architect of the 1880 rectory was inspired to produce an exuberant copycat design. The ornamental roof-tile pattern together with the timber-framing is perhaps a little excessive! The property is now a private residence.

HOPTON HEATH RAILWAY STATION   1912

Tobias Morgan was station-master here for five years from 1909, and he stands fourth from the left in his frock coat; his wife joins the group on the right wearing her white pinafore dress and blouse. Hopton Titterhill can be seen in the distance above the LNWR signal box, which was frequently 'switched out', ie not in use; it was demolished in 1945 and replaced with a ground frame solely to operate the points to the sidings. To the south are Bedstone Court, now a school, and Adley Level Crossing, the keeper's house of which survives. An interesting piece of railway furniture, a signal post accommodating three separate signals instructing traffic from both directions, was once located here. Perhaps this was an economy measure, but more likely it provided the best possible sight lines for locomen. There were also problems with the staggered platforms, which led to restrictions for passengers alighting from carriages which had come to a stop under the overbridge.

The former station-master's house, which has the date 1863 incorporated into the brickwork, thus confirming its build date, and the adjoining former booking office are now both private residences. The Pooley (a major railway supplier) weighbridge and hut is just out of the picture to the left; the hut now serves as a distinctive garden shed! Bert Morris, the weighbridge operator, is shown third from the left in shirt-sleeves, hand on hip. The station's former goods shed is now incorporated into a holiday village complex. The substantial boundary to the right is formed entirely of railway sleepers, all closely placed on end. The carpenter stands to the left of the photograph, and the porter in front of the booking office door, their names unknown.

Enquiries made locally of senior citizens emphatically confirm that this country station was often very busy, especially with freight movements. The cattle loading dock was frequently in use for transporting cattle and sheep away from Hopton. The farming community's requirement for animal feed also generated much business. Lastly, this rural area was the site of numerous ammunition dumps during World War II, and Hopton Heath goods yard was used for this dangerous and potentially explosive traffic.

2.10 Lydbury North – Home of the Walcots and Plowdens

ST MICHAEL AND ALL ANGELS   1924

Built of local rubble limestone with a pebbledash finish, St Michael's is a 12th century cruciform church with much interesting detail. Its recent past has been greatly influenced by the local Walcot and Plowden families, with their large mansions and estates within the parish. There are signs of Norman work in the nave and chancel windows. The west tower's proportions are substantial, the lower section being of the early 13th century, the battlemented highest points of the 17th and 19th. There must have been structural problems because massive buttresses were added in the early 16th century. There are six bells, two of which date from 1660. It has a late-medieval south porch, and the Jacobean pulpit is of 1624. The square transepts are known as the Plowden (north) and Walcot (south) chapels. Major but sympathetic restoration came late to Lydbury North, in fact, in the first decade of the 20th century. The work was carried out under the direction of J T Micklethwaite, its style conservative and totally in keeping with what is basically a Norman church.

VILLAGE SCENES – MULTI-VIEW   1919

This montage illustrating community life in Lydbury North 90 years ago is a deviation from photographer Heyworth's normal presentational style. Nevertheless, the postcard is full of interest. The images include the parish church; nearby Walcot Hall (erected in 1767 for Clive of India, replacing an earlier Elizabethan house); and the church school built in 1845 for 170 children, the successor to an earlier Free School which from 1662 had been held in the north transept of the church above the Walcot chapel. Other views of this once-important market town include a distant shot of the village from an adjoining hillside, and a village scene focusing on one of the timber-framed houses. Lydbury North is a reasonably-sized rural community and retains some necessary services; it still has a public house and community-run stores, but sadly has lost its sub-post office and is about to lose the school.

Chapter Three

The Hundred of Munslow

Church Stretton
Craven Arms
Stokesay

3.1 Church Stretton – Market Town and Spa

THE LONGMYND HOTEL   1910

Surrounded by trees on the hillside, this elaborate edifice was erected in 1900 as a 'hydro' – a hydropathic establishment. It was intended to cater for increasing numbers of visitors wanting to 'take the waters' of the area. The original pitched and extravagantly dormer-windowed roof has long since disappeared, to be replaced by the present flat roof. This grand 125-bedroomed building was a very ambitious project that was never destined to be even a modest success. The enterprise was not helped by the fact that the surrounding Stretton Hills did not have quantities of spa water containing the purported recuperative minerals. For a while quantities of spring water were imported by train from Llandrindod Wells. A plan to pipe water from Wentnor across the Stiperstones never materialised. The building was soon subject to a change of use and became a rather luxurious guesthouse, providing accommodation for the many visitors to this picturesque valley. In 1940, St Dunstan's, founded by Sir Arthur Pearson in 1915, moved to Church Stretton, utilising the hotel as its main base. The organisation had previously been centred at Ovingdean, Brighton, where it was obviously susceptible to enemy attack. Here in Church Stretton, specialist help was soon made available for the many war casualties, and training was provided for returning servicemen with seriously impaired sight in purpose-built workshops. The Longmynd Hotel eventually resumed normal business after the war.

3.2 Craven Arms and Stokesay – Railways and Sheep

PENLU HOUSE   1909

Situated on the Clun Road on the western perimeter of Craven Arms, this large Victorian house was occupied by members of the medical profession for at least 50 years. Dr Ernest Tredinnick, a prominent surgeon and physician who held numerous public health positions within the former Ludlow and Clun Unions, lived here from about 1895 to 1930. He and his family are pictured above. Aside from his professional life, the doctor was instrumental in the founding of Craven Arms Cricket Club. Penlu's next resident was Dr Cyril Hobson Flory, who lived here for many years and held very similar positions to his predecessor.

It seems unlikely that Heyworth produced only one postcard of Craven Arms. Surely, the two hotels and the railway station would have attracted his roving eye, but to date the author has not come across any other cards.

Lozenges, Tablets, Pills and Powders.

I. PILLS.

Head and Stomach	⎫ 3d. per dozen	Family Pills	⎫ 3d., 6d
Liver	⎪ pills	Digestive Pills	⎪ and
Compound Rhubarb	⎬ and in	Quinine Pills	⎬ 1/- boxes
Castor Oil	⎪ 6d. & 1/-	Blauds Pills	⎪
Little Liver Pills	⎭ boxes	1/- bottles	⎭

also in bottles   with pink white or gelatine coated.

Liver Granules—a special liver pills 9d. per bottle.

II. TABLETS.

Aspirins—Loose and 7½d., 10d, 11d. & 1/- packets all guaranteed makes. Good for Rheumatism and headaches.

Cascaras—6d. and 1/3 bottles, BW Tabloids 6d. and 1/8.

Ammoniated Quinine—a pleasant form in which to take this medicine.

Soda Mints—6d. bottles and loose, useful for flatulence, heartburn

Salicylate of Soda—a rheumatism remedy.

Chilblain Tablets—10d. per bottle, a good prepration for these troublesome things.

Clorate of Potash Pellets—4½ tins and loose, for sore throat. Do not take more than 3 daily

Compound Phenacetin Tablets—Very useful and safe for headaches.

Bismuth Pepsine and Charcoal—10d. and 1/6 for indigestion

Sutu Tablets—1/3 and 3/-, a fine tablet for poor digestion.

LOZENGES.

Ucal Bronchials—9d. and 1/6 tins. The little Lozenge that does a lot of good, excellent for coughs.

Allenbury's Glycerine, & Glycerine & Black Currant Pastilles—8d. and 1/3 per tin.

Ucapines 3d. per oz. Chestnuts 3d. per oz. Autopines (a jujube) 3d. per oz. Childrens Lozenges, 3d. oz. are all reliable.

48

74

Chapter Four

The Hundred of Wigmore

Burrington
Leintwardine
Brampton Bryan
Lingen
Walford
Adforton
Wigmore
Aymestrey
Nash (Titley)

4.1 Burrington – Tranquil Seclusion

CHURCH BANK   1912

Tucked away in the hills on the western edge of the Mortimer Forest and nestling alongside a tributary of the River Teme, is the small hamlet of Burrington. Little has changed since the photographer visited. The 150-year-old rustic cottages to the right stand opposite the parish church of St George. Completely rebuilt in 1855, it does, however, contain several earlier features including a 13th century octagonal font on a stem of four conjoined circular columns. Outside and at the east end of the church, are five rare 17th century cast-iron grave slabs, more than likely cast at nearby Bringewood Forge. The forge had been established in 1600, and was purchased by the Walker family in 1716. In 1727 Richard Knight from Madeley, East Shropshire, took over and considerably expanded the business. Iron ore was transported by horse and cart from the Clee Hills, and timber (the heat source) came from Deerfold, near Wigmore. Richard Knight died in 1745, and the iron grave slabs, interestingly etched with serif or sans serif lettering, are a memorial to him and four family members. The church can seat 80, and the register dates from 1541.

THE VICARAGE   1909

In 1862 George Frederick Bodley drew up plans for a new vicarage on the site of an existing inadequate 17ᵗʰ century cottage-style property. The result was a well-proportioned, attractive residence of dressed stone with numerous stone-mullioned windows, those to the gable ends being Gothic in style. With its tiled roof and harmonising stacks, the new vicarage – built at a cost of £1,230 – was certainly a success architecturally, but does come as a bit of a surprise in this secluded hamlet. No doubt it met with the approval of the Rev A E A S Scott, the privileged incumbent at the time of this photograph.

4.2 Leintwardine – Roman Bravinium

THE PARISH CHURCH OF ST MARY MAGDALENE   1912

This large church, standing high above the village, has several late 12ᵗʰ century characteristics, notably the former west doorway. The edifice is of local buff-coloured limestone. The stained glass is 19ᵗʰ century, but the west window in the north aisle and the lancets are all 14ᵗʰ century. As can be seen from the photograph, recent restoration had been carried out to the topmost battlemented segment of the tower. It is paler in colour, probably indicating maintenance work carried out in 1884 or 1894, similar work having previously been necessary in this area in 1865. Eight bells are installed, the last two being added in 1953. The register dates from 1547.

THE PARISH CHURCH OF ST MARY MAGDALENE INTERIOR   1912

Highlighted in this view of the interior of the parish church are the choir stalls, benches and misericords which are thought to have originated from Wigmore Abbey following the Dissolution of the Monasteries in the early 16th century. The five-bay south arcade, with its elegant round piers, is 13th century work. The church contains a striking monument by Peter Rouw dated 1835 to Sir Banastre Tarleton, a military man who fought in the American War of Independence. Born in Liverpool in 1754, Tarleton eventually became MP for that city in 1790. He also reached the exalted rank of major general in the army, and was a member of the House of Commons for all of 22 years. Created a baronet in 1815, he had by then already retired to live peacefully in Leintwardine, where he died on 25th January 1833.

Christmas card sent by the vicar J.W. Colvin 1912.

LEINTWARDINE HOUSE   1911

Situated off the High Street, 1814 was the the date when retired General Sir Banastre Tarleton and his wife, Lady Susan, took up the tenancy from the then owner, William Edwards. It is suspected that the interior walls of the house were soon decorated with the spoils of war, for many trophies were brought back to England by the new tenant. Banastre Tarleton's military career had begun when he purchased a commission as a cornet in the 1st Regiment of the King's Dragoon Guards, a heavy cavalry regiment. Having volunteered for overseas duty, by 1776 he found himself in America fighting numerous battles in the eastern and southern states, as the American War of Independence ebbed and flowed. During the next two and half hectic years, he rose from the lowest commissioned officer rank to that of lieutenant-colonel.

Tarleton enjoyed appreciable success during his five-year American adventure, and brought back to this country several wonderful mementoes of battle, in particular, the captured regimental standards of defeated American regiments. In 2006 these colours, having survived for over 200 years, were offered for sale at Sotheby's, New York, by a descendant of Tarleton. One of them – the silk battle flag of the 2nd Connecticut Dragoons, taken in 1779 – was to achieve the princely sum of £6.7 million.

Other notable occupants of this desirable property were: Colonel John Colvin (1848), who supposedly planted the Wellingtonia tree in the garden to commemorate the birth a few years earlier, in 1841, of his daughter, Elizabeth (known as Bessie); although Wellingtonias were only introduced into this country in 1853. Sir Henry Meredyth Plowden (1896); George Jebb (1911), who converted the stables and made alterations to the rear entrance and drive; and Colonel F J Scott (1947). The cantilevered stone staircase is very much the focal point of the house interior.

It is interesting to note the remuneration of staff employed at the house in 1906-8: the gardener's wage was £1 per week, the cook's salary £24 per year, and that of the kitchen maid £5 per year.

Portrait of Sir Banastre Tarleton

The colours of Colonel Abraham Buford's Virginia troops (left) captured at Waxsaws in 1780 and (right) the colours of Colonel Sheldon's Connecticut dragoons captured at Westchester County, New York, in 1779.

THE WAR MEMORIAL   1921

The new cemetery at Leintwardine was opened in 1901, but it was obviously not until after the First World War that this ornate memorial was erected in the cemetery grounds, the cost being met by public subscription. The memorial is inscribed with 35 names, honouring those men of the neighbourhood who fell in the 1914-18 War; a further five names of those who perished in the Second World War were added later.

THE VILLAGE SCHOOL   1912

History relates that Leintwardine's first school was set up in 1659, no doubt followed by numerous other small fee-paying establishments. The first endowed school, together with a master's house, was erected in 1845 by local builder, Richard Baxter Prince, to accommodate 200 children. An extension of 1871 provided places for a further 20 pupils. Education in Victorian times often relied on unqualified assistants and so-called pupil monitors, as there were always insufficient qualified teachers available. School fees were two old pence per week in mid-Victorian times. The master's wife and infants' mistress, Mrs Enos Charnock, planted an oak tree in the grounds in 1906 which had been grown from an acorn first sown in 1897, the year of Queen Victoria's Silver Jubilee. A new Church of England Endowed Primary School was opened in Watling Street in 1973, and the former school premises, portrayed above, now serve as a community centre.

THE RIVER TEME BRIDGE   1912

The Romans must have explored suitable sites for crossing the Teme in the 1st and 2nd centuries AD. Initially, the crossing would have been at the river's shallowest point in the form of a ford, later superseded by a simple timber structure. By the 17th century a narrow stone-built bridge probably existed. The current, pleasing five-arched limestone bridge at Leintwardine originated in the 18th century. The confluence of the Rivers Teme and Clun just a short distance upstream has caused numerous floods in the past, partially as a result of the bridge's restriction of water flow. Extensive repairs due to flood damage were necessary in 1915 and 1929, and the bridge was widened in 1930.

THE PLOUGH, HIGH STREET   1912

This scene outside The Plough takes one back to the time when the road was still only a dirt track. Situated at the top of High Street, the attractively thatched property dates from the 17th century, but its name derives from the period it served as an inn during the mid-19th century; Samuel Evans was the landlord. By the 1870s it had become a farmhouse. In the early days, there was a holding reservoir sourced from Buckton Park in the vicinity, and it was from here that the lower portion of the village was supplied with water. The Kirby family farmed the Plough holding for much of the 20th century. Incidentally, the first agricultural trades union in Great Britain was established in Leintwardine; its first meeting was held in 1871, and it was formally registered on 24th June 1873 as the Leintwardine Co-operative and Industrial Society.

CHURCH STREET POST OFFICE   1912

These premises at 15 Church Street were purpose-built by David Fairbank and his wife, Sarah (née Overton). Sarah had been sub-postmistress at various different locations in Leintwardine from the 1870s. She had married David Fairbank, the local veterinary, in 1897, and together they established these joint premises opposite the church. Sarah's well-stocked stores appear to include an array of picture postcards displayed in the front window; David's surgery was nextdoor. Sarah was a Methodist Society steward for 40 years from 1898; her husband was also a Methodist follower, being a lay preacher. David fetched the mail and papers from Bucknell Railway Station each morning on behalf of his wife. Sarah continued as sub-postmistress for 63 years until her death in 1938 at the age of 84. David died in 1940. In 1942, Miss Alice Harriet Wadeley, previously assistant to Sarah, having purchased the business, transferred the post office to her own house, Fern Cottage, nextdoor. Here, she was assisted by her sister, Florence Snowdrop, and later by Miss Janet Hayes and Mrs Deanna Watkins.

HIGH STREET   1922

Another nicely-composed image recording life in the High Street soon after World War I. Bright sunshine and the resultant shadows are a bonus. The grocer's shop to the right, once the Old Court House, was established in 1768. Taken over by a Mr Griffiths in 1841, Richard Price was the next proprietor in 1856, followed by a Mr Oliver, and Charles Sadler in 1902. Alfred Hopkins was behind the counter in 1922 and he continued in business for 20 years. Don Faulkner took over circa 1950s, others followed but unfortunately, like many other village stores, competition from larger retailers eventually ensured its closure. It is now a private residence. The inverted horseshoe sign on the left advertises the Leintwardine premises of the Stokesay and Craven Arms Garage Company.

LANGFORD'S THE BUTCHER'S, WATLING STREET   1912

This photograph provides a superb record of Langford's butcher's shop. The owner, Richard Langford, stands in the doorway, knife in hand; his bearded assistant holds a sharpening steel; in-between sits a well-nourished butcher's dog; carcasses are left hanging exposed to the elements. Nowadays this would be deemed a health and safety nightmare! The array includes a whole pig and sides of beef, whilst on the half-beast to the left is displayed a printed card showing that it had won 2nd prize at Jackson & McCartney's recent Craven Arms sale. Cattle successfully bid for at Craven Arms market were driven to Leintwardine, a distance of eight miles, where they were slaughtered and prepared for sale in the slaughterhouse next to the butcher's shop. The sausages were said to be of prime quality, (well bread)!

WATLING STREET   1909

Edwardian quietude at its very best! This is one of several photographs taken by Heyworth along the length of Watling Street. A well-turned out horse and trap pauses outside the Swan Hotel; alongside, a soldier home on leave poses with a few locals. The Swan at this time was run by Mrs Susan Crowther; the premises were closed down in the 1990s. The wall on the left is that of the erstwhile vicarage, and further up the street is the post office. It is evident that the road surface was hardly fit for the newly-introduced motor car; it has yet to receive its first coat of tarmacadam, and the kerbing of roughly-laid setts does its best to delineate the footpath.

THE LION HOTEL   1919

Attractively placed just below the confluence of the Teme and the Clun, and alongside the bridge, the Lion Hotel is highly unlikely to have been the first building on this site. It has been suggested that the name originated from nearby Downton, where a beer-house called The Lion closed in the early 1800s. Assisted by a vigorous advertising campaign, this family hotel and posting house attracted a steady flow of guests including fishermen, cyclists, walkers and general tourists. Surviving play-bills show that theatrical troupes performed within the precincts of the hotel in the 1840s. Trade was also boosted by the numerous race meetings, May Fairs and street markets held in the vicinity. In the 1940s, apart from enjoying a natter over a pint in the bar, local residents could also practise the art of fishing on a one-mile stretch of the Clun for the tidy sum of five shillings per day. It is said that the Leintwardine Fishing Club, founded in 1811 by James Ackers, was the very first such club formed in England, and meetings were held at The Lion, a place of great conviviality. Major G C Alletson was the proprietor in the 1920s, and he was always quick to extol its attractions, especially the fishing. In the 1970s it was well worth making a special journey to The Lion just to sample their superlative carved buffets!

THE CONGREGATIONAL CHAPEL   1912

Situated in Tipton's Lane towards the north of the village, its polygonal apse faces the camera, and the elegant bell turret of the chapel lies to the east. Of rubble with yellow and blue brick dressings, the edifice was erected in 1870, with the energetic backing of Edward Halsey of Hightree House. The first minister was the Rev W D Ingham, followed by his son, the Rev Ernest Ingham, in 1887. The chapel had seating for 200, and the adjacent schoolroom 60 places.

HIGHTREE HOUSE 1910

Hightree House was probably built in the late-18th century. However, Edward Halsey, the owner in 1870, made significant additions in that year. A large country house which has seen many changes over the years, it is architecturally complicated with numerous gables, projecting two-storied bays, and a twin-columned entrance porch. Originally a compact and manageable gentleman's residence, it became a VAD (Voluntary Aid Detachment) Hospital during World War I, a guest house in the 1920s and '30s, and was requisitioned as the local RAOC headquarters in World War II. In 1948, Haydn Thomas purchased the property and gave it a new lease of life as a preparatory school. Initially, 149 pupils were catered for, boarding and tuition fees being 15 guineas per pupil per term. The school closed in July 1961 and the property sold for £5,750. It was later renamed by a property developer to Leintwardine Manor and is now divided into privately-owned apartments.

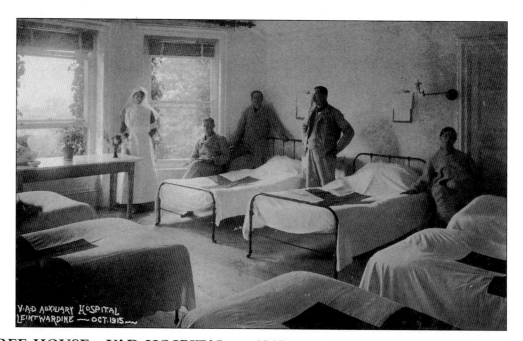

HIGHTREE HOUSE – VAD HOSPITAL 1915

A caring volunteer nurse poses with her patients in what is obviously one of the larger wards within the main body of Hightree House. There were other smaller units erected in the grounds. Whilst the shot is obviously posed, the room is immaculate, with Red Cross bed covers much in evidence. The vases of flowers are a nice homely touch, and surely the ambience must have had a positive effect on the convalescence of patients, distracting their thoughts from the horrors of the Flanders trenches, which had brought them here.

HIGHTREE HOUSE – VAD HOSPITAL   1915

Another in a series of photographs taken by Robert Newton Heyworth at Hightree House during the time it was in use as a World War I hospital. A proud Miss Crawshay (centre) the then owner, stands on the steps at the front of her home with nursing staff and patients. As was usual with these Red Cross hospitals, patients would have come from many different regiments, representing many Allied countries; soldiers from France and Belgium, as well as Great Britain and the Commonwealth, would have been cared for at Leintwardine. They would probably have suffered comparatively minor injuries and would be convalescing. Shell-shock was a relatively frequent problem, as was 'trench foot', caused by continually standing in water in the trenches. It is a sobering thought that many soldiers such as those shown here would have been sent back to the battlefields of France. Who knows their fate? Miss Gertrude Helen Crawshay, a wonderful benefactor, died on 14th October 1932 aged 70. She is buried in Leintwardine Cemetery, and is fondly remembered by the chapel which bears her name in the parish church.

4.3 Brampton Bryan – Home of the Harleys

THE BRON FAIR (1)   1906

The Horse Fair at Brampton Bryan, always known as the Bron Fair, was held in the main street of the village on the 22nd June each year. All other business, hereabouts, would come to a standstill for the day; horse-dealers, farmers and travellers would spend the time buying and selling horses, together with the associated tack – harnesses, bridles and saddles. Everyone would dress up in their Sunday best, and the wearing of a hat appeared to be obligatory.

THE BRON FAIR (2)   1912

Yet another busy scene, full of activity! The bar at the rear of the blacksmith's shop appears to be a rather busy spot, with thirsty folk queuing for refreshments. Meanwhile, a farmer in the foreground shows off his pony to an interested buyer, with a successful seller counting his money just behind them. A vintage stock lorry is seen in the centre background, no doubt waiting to transport some new purchases. Two policemen, centre left, wearing forage-type hats, keep a watchful eye on proceedings. Here again, everyone wears a hat.

BRAMPTON BRYAN CASTLE RUINS   1934

This 12th century motte and bailey castle was extensively rebuilt in the 14th century. In 1294, Bryan de Brampton's daughter, Margaret, married Robert Harley. The descendants of this union have inherited the castle for 22 generations. An amazing fact: virtually 700 years of continuous family ownership! In 1643, during the early stages of the Civil War, Royalist forces attacked the castle whilst Sir Robert Harley MP was away in London on parliamentary business. It was left to his third wife, Brilliana, to organise resistance. A meagre defence force of 50 villagers and 50 Roundheads, led by a Sergeant Hakluyt, bravely withstood the siege by 600 Royalist Cavaliers for a period of six weeks. A few weeks later Lady Brilliana was to die – succumbing, it is said, to a cold. The castle was taken a year later, sacked, never to be rebuilt.

BRAMPTON BRYAN HALL   1910

Brampton Bryan is mentioned in the Domesday Book. Following the sacking of the castle and church in the Civil War, it was the church that was rebuilt first by the Harleys, followed by a new residence in the 1660s. A little of this building survives to the rear of the existing house, and the former dungeons of the ruined castle are also partly incorporated. The present building (circa 1790) is an imposing example of Georgian architecture. This large mansion of pale red brick is symmetrical in plan; the high pedimented frontage is of seven bays, the central three being placed forward for emphasis. Prominent stone quoins with alternate bonding are a noticeable feature, and sash windows proliferate over the three storeys. The south elevation has a neat porch with twin Roman Doric columns and balustraded roof; there are also full-length pilasters to this elevation.

Did you know that this area of North Herefordshire is well represented in streets of the capital city? For instance, London W1 includes Harley Street and Wigmore Street, familiar names to local inhabitants!

4.4   Lingen – Betwixt the Hills

LINGEN HALL   1910

Surrounded by trees in a secluded area to the south-east of the village lies Lingen Hall, a 12 bed-roomed Georgian-style house which was built in the mid-1850s. The owners were Joseph and Mary Gisborne who were from Allestree Hall, South Derbyshire. The house was the centre of a 541-acre estate of several tenant farms and cottages, plus 100 acres of woodland. Effingham House School from Leatherhead, Surrey, was evacuated here lock, stock and barrel for the duration of World War II. The estate was later sold to Charles Chetwynd Talbot, Earl of Shrewsbury. In 1957, the estate was broken up and individual lots sold mainly to the tenants. However, Sir Alfred Nicholas privately purchased the Hall, together with a seven-acre land holding.

LINGEN, THE DAIRY FARM   1910

Once part of Home Farm on the Lingen Hall Estate, a purpose-built milking parlour and ancillary buildings were erected circa 1900, and specialised machinery purchased – all associated with the establishment of a pedigree herd of Jersey cows. Mr Burton was the herdsman in charge, and he lived in the adjoining farmhouse until the 1920s. It was a busy and productive enterprise, milk being taken twice daily by horse and cart to Bucknell Railway Station for onward transmission to the big cities.

LINGEN, THE VILLAGE INN AND COTTAGES   1925

The Royal George Inn appears to have had a recent make-over, including a new trellis-sided porch and a coat of paint to its brickwork. Interestingly, this is another local hostelry taking its name from the gunship built for George II and his adventures against the Spanish. The adjoining 17th century square timber-framed cottages also appear to be in prime condition externally. All this, of course, for the benefit of the photographer! Now known as Ivy and Rose Cottages, they have in recent times been used for agricultural workers.

4.5 Walford – Pastoral Crossing

WALFORD HAMLET   1922

Walford is a small community on the main road from Leintwardine to Knighton, where the highway divides for Buckton, Adforton and Lingen. The Court House has incorporated into its structure two capitals of the 12th and 13th century, more than probably pickings from nearby Wigmore Abbey. North-west of Walford Farm is a Bronze Age round barrow, nine feet high and 94 feet in diameter.

4.6 Adforton – Abbot's Retreat

ADFORTON VILLAGE   1912

Situated between its bigger neighbours Leintwardine and Wigmore, Adforton has been very much affected by progress, more particularly by the advent of the motor car. In Edwardian days and before, life here was centred on agriculture, with everything moving at a sedate pace. The gradual increase in traffic soon led to a widening of the highway and the removal of acute corners and other hazards. Adforton must have suffered more than many other villages in this respect, but conversely there has been little or no growth. The small parish church of St Andrew, out of shot to the right, is of local Mocktree Hill limestone, built to a design by J P Seddon and completed in 1875. It now serves a dual purpose, both as a place of worship and as a community centre. The house to the left and marked with an 'x' near eaves-level was the village shop. On the back of the postcard, the sender explains that the blind lady at the shop had recently fallen downstairs and been burnt to death. The exact correlation of circumstances is not known, but it was obviously a most unfortunate occurrence. Adforton remains a retiring village with little or no signs of development.

4.7 Wigmore – Stronghold of Marcher Lords

WIGMORE CASTLE RUINS 1919

Nothing much remains of the original castle of William FitzOsbern, the Earl of Hereford. Heyworth must have had a bit of a scramble, camera slung on his back, up past the church to get to the ruins from the Castle Inn on the main street. This view is not achievable today, as the castle has been overwhelmed by trees and impenetrable undergrowth. How much better it was as seen here, with grassy banks and a few specimen trees! The castle was the property of the Mortimers, kinsmen of William the Conqueror, until the 15th century. The inner bailey is surrounded by towers of the late 13th and 14th centuries, its gatehouse half-buried, whilst in the north-west corner is situated the oval keep. Much of what survives today is 14th century work; by the 16th century, the castle was already in a sorry state of decay.

Tradition has it that during the Civil War, Brilliana, wife of the then owner, Sir Robert Harley of Brampton Bryan, hastened the castle's demise by dismantling much of what remained of the defences. This she did in the hope of stopping the Royalist Cavalier forces from using Wigmore as a fortified base in their raids against her husband's property at Brampton Bryan. Extensive stabilisation of the fabric was carried out in 1999.

THE VILLAGE STREET 1920

A delightful, unspoilt village on a slight incline. The parish church of St James is set amongst trees at a higher elevation on the narrow road leading to the castle. There are numerous interesting houses around the main crossroads at the top of the village; these are both of brick dating to the 17th century and timber-framed of the same period. St James's parish church is early Norman in origin with numerous medieval features, and was restored sympathetically in 1864 by G F Bodley. Wigmore Abbey (in Adforton parish) was founded in 1179 by Hugh Mortimer for Augustinian canons. What is now referred to as the Abbot's Lodgings is the main surviving building, full of reminders of the 14th and 15th centuries, more particularly windows and their tracery, substantial roof-framing including trusses and collar beams, and a complementary gateway.

4.8 Aymestrey – Centurion's Way

THE CROWN INN 1911

The street bunting is out, almost certainly in celebration of King George V's Coronation on 22nd June 1911. C W Bassett was then the landlord of the pub, now renamed The Riverside Inn because of its proximity to the River Lugg. It is a popular watering hole alongside Watling Street, the old Roman road running south between Bravinium (Leintwardine) and Isca Silurium (Caerleon), near Newport in South Wales. Carts and drays of every description stand outside the property nextdoor, but no horses are in evidence; most likely, they had not conveyed customers to the inn, but were awaiting repair by Acton Farmer, the local wheelwright, believed to have premises adjoining The Crown. The copings to the wing wall of the river bridge make a pleasant resting place for the gentleman in the picture; he will not be missing much of what might be going on! The bridge was built to the design of John Gethin of nearby Kingsland after the great flood of 1795. It was significantly widened and improved by County Council engineers in 1931.

POST OFFICE AND VILLAGE SHOP 1925

The Cole family managed the village shop and post office for a number of decades, Mrs Sarah Cole being the sub-postmistress here as early as 1900. The small sow and piglet appear to be gleaning scraps, perhaps dropped by customers as they were leaving the shop down the well-worn steps. They appear to be free-range animals, in spite of the fact that the motor car was by this time making an impact even on our country roads.

Visitors to the district might like to consider the steady walk to Croft Ambrey, an Iron Age fort nearly two miles to the north-east of the parish church. It is spectacular, the inner enclosure alone being of some eight acres, surrounded by a series of three ramparts and two ditches. Excavated finds suggest that the Romans also understood its strategic importance, and utilised the position for military purposes. The view from the Scots pine-covered knoll on the public footpath eventually leading to Croft Castle and overlooking Yatton, Leinthall Earls and distant Wigmore to the north-west is a fitting reward for the walker's endeavours.

4.9 Nash (Titley) – Once a Country Junction

NASH QUARRY DELIVERY 1914

It is not difficult to imagine photographer Heyworth on his way to some assignment, perhaps at nearby Presteigne, unexpectedly stumbling upon this elderly character with his donkey cart. He must have immediately realised the potential of such an image, and politely asked if the waggoner would mind stopping to have his photograph taken. It is assumed that the donkeys are four-in-hand, and will have their work cut out 'tushing' this heavy load of quarry stone any great distance. After all, it is rather undulating country around here! If the load is not for local use on housing, highway or river bank, it is very likely that the stone is destined for either Titley Junction or Presteigne railway station for onward transmission much further afield.

Old Radnor limestone quarry.

Chapter Five

The Hundred of Stretford

Eardisland
Pembridge

5.1 Eardisland – Riverside Charm

VIEW FROM THE BRIDGE   1913

This tranquil scene on the River Arrow looks somewhat unfamiliar today. The picturesque village of Eardisland is acclaimed for its black-and-white houses and cottages, 14th century Staick House, and its 17th century red-bricked, four-gabled dovecote. The bridge on which the photographer stands was built in 1799 by civil engineer John Gethin of nearby Kingsland. It replaced an earlier wooden bridge, and cost was £379. This new bridge was only 12 feet wide, and most likely endured horse and cart and even motor traffic without major incident until the Second World War. The American Army was stationed hereabouts, and a lorry convoy failed miserably to negotiate its narrow confines successfully. As a result, much of the parapet stonework landed up in the river. The bridge was widened to 24 feet in 1945 at a cost of £1,000. The Arrow has been dammed downstream from here to create a holding pond for the nearby Georgian Old Mill and Mill House. On the south side of the river is the 12th century church of St Mary the Virgin.

5.2 Pembridge – Historically Good-Looking

THE CHURCH OF ST MARY THE VIRGIN (1)   1925

The parish church lies partly hidden behind the 16th century open Market Hall. The visitor is immediately struck by the unusual detached bell tower with huge corner posts dendro-dated to the 13th century, an irregular octagonal lower stone storey and high pyramidal roof, topped by a weather-boarded bell-stage and slender spirelet. Internally, massive timberwork cannot fail to impress. Apparently, the structure and design owe much to Scandinavian thinking, and the Pembridge example is one of seven detached belfries in Herefordshire. There are five bells which were recast and retuned in 1898. The bell-house was last restored in 1983-84. A chiming clock was placed here in 1891 in memory of Rev J F Crouch. This 13th and 14th century church was no doubt built on a Norman foundation, although there is little visual evidence of this, just two built-up 12th century arches in the chancel.

ST MARY THE VIRGIN – INTERIOR (2)   1925

Large and well-lit, the interior of the church is inviting with its tall six-bay arcades, the lack of pews creating an overall feel of spaciousness. Most of this work is of 1320-60. At the time of the photograph, the edifice was lit by pleasing hanging oil lamps and ornate brass chandeliers of 1722. The unusual square font is 13th century. The carved panel in the reader's desk at the end of the choir stalls possibly dates from the same period; the pulpit and lectern are Jacobean, as is the altar rail – all with dragon motifs. The church contains numerous tomb chests, and the register dates from 1564.

THE MARKET SQUARE AND NEW INN   1925

Pretty, black-and-white framing abounds in this enchanting North Herefordshire village. Heyworth would have been delighted with the variety of photographic shots presented; he may even have drawn a shooting analogy: Pembridge is like a pheasant shoot: when a flush of pheasants fly over, it is difficult to know which one to shoot first! It has been a market town since Henry de Pennebrugge was granted a weekly market and two annual fairs by charter in 1240. The Annual Fair on 15th May was charmingly and pertinently called the Cowslip Fair, and six months later the November fair was known as the Woodcock Fair. Both were hiring fairs, when agricultural workers would wait around the market place, offering their services to farmers for the forthcoming year. The mid-16th century hip-roofed open Market Hall, placed centre stage in this picture has eight carved oak supporting posts and was likely to have been thatched originally. The large stone to the left of the building is a 'nail stone', where deals were struck and 'paid on the nail'. The black-and-white half-timbered building to the right is Church House; its early use is thought to have been that of a school. The New Inn fills the background and is a building of early 17th century date.

A TYPICAL PEMBRIDGE STREET SCENE   1913

The setting shows three hotels, all in close proximity to one another: Jessie Davies' Queen's Head, with its good stabling, stands to the right; Ye Olde Steppes shop is a little further to the right and the red-bricked Red Lion Inn, where Sam Boulter once filled the jugs, yet further beyond; in the centre background is the timber-framed New Inn, formerly known as Cooke's Public House. A courthouse, built in 1311, had previously occupied the site but was burnt down. Tradition has it that following the Battle of Mortimer's Cross in 1461, the victorious Edward, Earl of the Marches (Edward IV) and his defeated opponents Owen and Jasper Tudor, who had led the Lancastrians' attack from Wales, were later to meet here at the New Inn to sign a peace treaty.

EAST STREET   1934

A tranquil village scene with a Ford T Tourer parked up on the right, just before the sweet shop. The rendered building with a slightly jettied first-floor frontage, pictured to the left, is of much interest; it is the 16th century Greyhound Inn which at this time was hiding its splendid close-set vertical timbers and carved brackets. It was named not after a breed of dog, but more ingeniously after the Greyhound horse-drawn coach which once ran between London and Birmingham. The building has since been renovated, its timbers exposed, and it has also witnessed a change of name and function. It is now a licensed restaurant called The King's House. The blacksmith and wheelwright had premises just beyond, where the gable of the black-and-white property juts out to the right. A terrace of attractive timber-framed cottages stands to the left rear, and it was from one of these that the all-important district nurse operated at this time.

STATION ROAD   1913

With his back to Ye Olde Steppes shop, Heyworth directs his camera lens down Station Road. On the right, somewhat unusually for Pembridge, is a redbrick building, The Queen's Head Hotel, likely to be early 19th century. The timber-framed almshouses on the left were built in 1661 for the poor women of the neighbourhood by benefactor Bryan Duppa, Bishop of Winchester. On the wall is a plaque which reads: *Forget not your good benefactor Brion Duppa, Bishop of Winchester who bielded this hospitoll in 1661.* As the street name suggests, the Great Western Railway Station was a short distance away, an intermediate stop on the branch line from Leominster to Kington, Presteigne and New Radnor. The line had closed completely by 1964. Readers may be interested to know that the sender of this postcard has ink-marked the gable end of the last cottage on the left and noted tantalisingly: *"This is where the murder was done."*

Chapter Six

The Hundred of Huntington

6.1 Kington – Ancient Market Town

PARISH CHURCH OF ST MARY MAGDALENE   1922

It seems that Robert Newton Heyworth travelled no further south into Herefordshire than the market town of Kington and nearby Pembridge. Situated to the west of the town centre and on a hillside, St Mary's is a large church built circa 1200 of grey stone, the oldest element being the spectacular and virtually detached south tower with its quadrilateral, three-tiered broach spire, within which are housed six bells; this striking pyramidal feature was restored in 1794. An external staircase was added in 1885. The chancel is a grand structure of circa 1225, with numerous lancet windows. The nave was completely rebuilt to its present majesty about a century later. The font is Norman with zig-zag and rope moulding

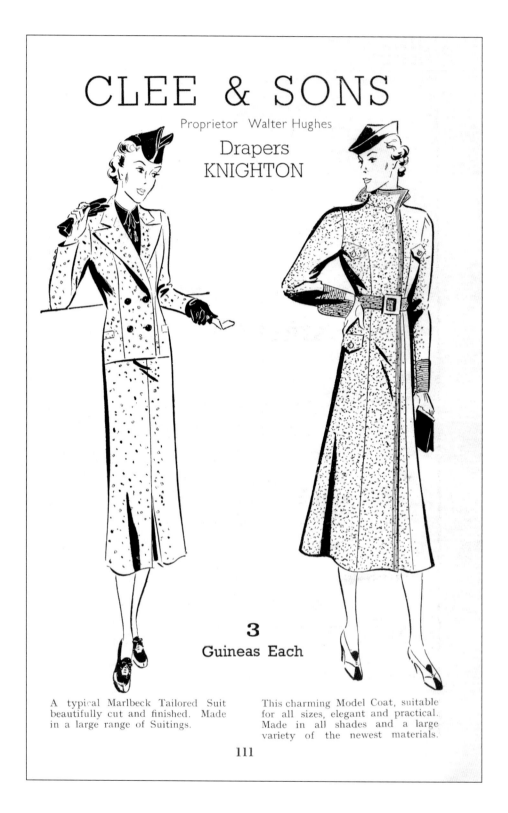

CLEE & SONS

Proprietor Walter Hughes

Drapers
KNIGHTON

3
Guineas Each

A typical Marlbeck Tailored Suit beautifully cut and finished. Made in a large range of Suitings.

This charming Model Coat, suitable for all sizes, elegant and practical. Made in all shades and a large variety of the newest materials.

111

Chapter Seven

The Hundred of Knighton

Knighton
Stanage
Knucklas and Heyope
Lloyney
Beguildy and Felindre

7.1 Knighton – Tref-Y-Clawdd – Ancient Borough

THE PARISH CHURCH AND MILL GREEN   1909

St Edward's is probably the fourth church to have stood on this particular site, but only the 14th century west tower is left to remind us of previous edifices. Its reconstructed pyramidal bell-stage forms a neat reassuring cap. The main body of the church was rebuilt in 1752, and again in 1877 by S Pountney Smith, the Munslow-born architect, at an overall cost of £3,750. At that time there were insufficient funds to pay for work required on the chancel, and it was not until 1897 that this essential restoration was completed, the architect being J L Pearson. The result is thought to be a sympathetic piece of work. The church is of random local stone, probably from the Kinsley Wood Quarry, and stands proudly and majestically just north of the town, alongside the River Teme.

A KNIGHTON WEDDING   1912

It is all top hat and tails, fancy millinery and elegant dresses! And why not, for this is the wedding on 26th September 1912 of Miss Nesta Faith Green Price to William Humphrey Williams. The couple are about to leave the vicarage in an Edwardian car on their way to Norton Manor, the bride's family home. The motor is a 1908 Renault Limousine, one of the very first completely enclosed motor cars. It bears the Radnorshire registration number FO 219 and was provided for the occasion by Mr Bootes of Gwernaffle, near Knighton.

CHURCH STREET CORNER 1930

This view from the top of Church Street shows the cobbled descent to St Edward's Church. It captures what remained of Chandos on the left, and the ecclesiastical-looking Barclays Bank on the right. The Chandos, originally a rather splendid property which boasted a pillared porch with street-side railings, was the town house of the Brydges family, later Dukes of Chandos. However, with the advent of the motor car, much of its frontage was demolished, and the road widened in 1931. At the time of this photograph, David Davies had his butcher's shop in one half of the truncated Chandos, and a temperance hotel (with its entrance just around the corner) used the other half. The site of the bank was once occupied by The Duke's Arms, a hostelry which closed in 1831; later W J Lewis's draper's shop, and then the Birmingham and Counties Bank were located here. The premises were demolished and rebuilt as Barclays Bank in 1892. The parish church, seen in the distance, is dedicated to St Edward, believed to be the only such dedication in the whole of Wales.

HAMAR'S SHOP, MARKET STREET   1919

Mr Hamar appears to have organised things to perfection for this photograph. The proprietor of the Market Street shop stands to the left, whilst his staff, all suitably dressed for work, are spread out along the shop frontage next to his pride and joy, the delightful Ford Model T delivery van. Apparently, tea and coffee were Mr Hamar's specialities, and staff must have spent much time extracting these commodities from large chests, weighing them and putting them into quarter- pound packets. Skinning large cheeses would have been another time-consuming task. The local farming community was catered for with the usual bar soaps, block salt, treacle, jams and a large choice of other provisions. Mr Hamar would almost certainly have had his own bakery, so bread and cakes would have been on offer.

W. HAMAR & SONS

Wholesale and Family Grocers
Tea and Coffee Specialists   :
Provision Merchants   :   :
Flour and Corn Dealers :   :

Home-cured Danish and Canadian Bacon
and Hams.   Sliced by Berkel Machine

REGULAR MOTOR DELIVERIES
TO ALL PARTS

ESTABLISHED   TELEPHONE 35
SIXTY YEARS   RING US UP

Market Street, KNIGHTON
RADNORSHIRE

115

PHILLIPS'S SHOP, THE NARROWS   1914

Bill Phillips' shop in the Narrows at Knighton contained a real assortment of goods to attract potential customers. Inside the front window gramophone records are on show, but outside is stacked the real surprise: up to 70 large baskets full of whimberries await collection by railway waggoner, John Davies. The proprietor stands at the shop entrance looking well-pleased with himself, perhaps in anticipation of the forthcoming financial windfall. The destination of the whimberries is not the market place, but Lancashire cotton towns where they will be used to dye naval uniforms. The asking price for whimberries at this time would have been 6^d per pound; but later during the First World War, as demand increased, the price would have risen sharply to 2/6^d per pound.

THE NARROWS   1918

The Narrows, an extension of High Street, is said to date back to the Tudor period. It was an extremely busy area of town, where traders worked in cramped and difficult conditions. Aptly named, this steep cobbled street must have been horrendous in stormy or snowy conditions. Imagine the problems resulting from rain-water cascading down from the top, or from a layer of snow covering the surface: there is no surface water drainage. J L Allcock and his son, Charles, are busy in their bakery and grocery shop on the left, where they display hams, butter at 2/- per pound and numerous freshly-baked loaves. Lewis's shoe shop is on the right, with Ernie Tudge's grocery store a little below and opposite where the two boys are standing. Rees Jones has his draper's sign just below and to the left, whilst G M Perkins' chemist shop was a short distance further on. Ross's of Leominster had a shoe shop just below to the right. Chaos reigned here when on the wet cobbles John Davies (alias John the Dray) arrived on his rounds to and from the railway station. Stopping and starting on the slippery slope, and avoiding the miscellaneous shop-front displays, needed skilful horsemanship.

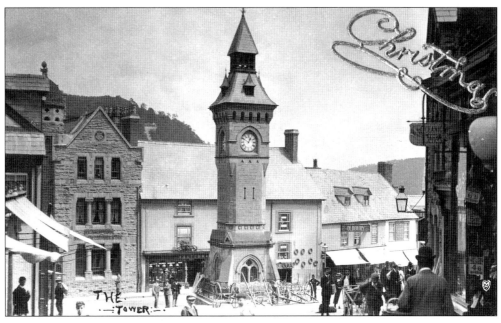

THE CLOCK TOWER   1907

This Christmas card would surely have arrived too late to convey the intended Christmas greetings, as it was not posted until 9ᵖᵐ on 24ᵗʰ December, though there were Christmas Day deliveries in those days. The clock indicates that it is a little after midday, and the market is evidently in progress. The clock tower was built on the site of the former town hall and assembly rooms, which also used to house the police station and cells. In 1872, Mr Thomas Moore of the Old Hall, Llanfihangel-Rhydithon, eight miles south-west from Knighton on the road to Penybont and Rhayader, provided the finance for this landmark structure. The architects were Haddon Bros from Hereford, also the home of the builders, Welsh & Son. It is now a Grade II listed building and has recently been renovated. The clock tower is surrounded by buck-rakes, mowers and seed drills, and no doubt the policeman is thinking there is too much stuff cluttering up the street! Oldbury's the printers have a display of postcards to the right, whilst Ross's are selling their boots for 6/11d. Those were the days!

THE MAY FAIR   1910

The May Fair in Knighton was always a very special occasion, not only for those thousands of locals attending, but also for the travelling folk with their specialised fun-fair machinery. The Gotheimers brought their Giant Roundabout and various sideshows, the Farrells their Gallopers; and the numerous attractions of Marshall Hill who hailed from Bedminster Down, Bristol, were there for all to enjoy. They and others pitched up in various positions in and around the town, all ready for a 17th May start. There were swing-boats, cakewalks, boxing booths, waxworks, hoopla, a Wild West show, shooting galleries, coconut shies and several merry-go-rounds, together with assorted smaller sideshows. Catchpennies selling absolutely everything were dotted between the entertainment rides. The roads were teeming with horse and traps, bicycles, motorcycles and a few early motorcars. Everyone wore their Sunday best: stiff-collared shirts and suits for the men, pretty bonnets and flowing dresses for the ladies, and polished black boots and caps for the boys. Those that were determined to join in the fun came from every village and hamlet in the surrounding area. They clambered over stiles, making their way down country lanes from farms and smallholdings high up in the hills. Some maintained that even the closest neighbours did not see each other from one May Fair to the next. The fair-goers were met by noisy, dynamo-powered showman's steam engines which did their best to provide lighting and electricity for every conceivable item of equipment from gallopers and steam yachts to the mysteriously evocative fairground organ. Everyone was intent on enjoying the event, especially the schoolchildren who were allowed a day off for the second day of the Fair.

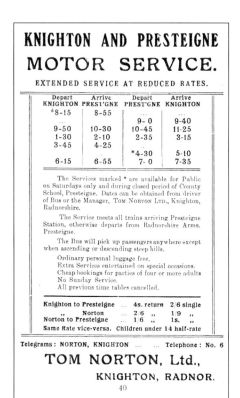

KNIGHTON TOWN BAND, BROAD STREET   1912

The Knighton Town Band lead the long procession of floats to the show field. On the left is the ashlar-faced Norton Arms and adjoining Assembly Rooms, built on behalf of Richard Green Price of Norton Manor in 1867. In this building was held the Annual Gala Dinner and Ball, and it still functions as a hotel today. The Assembly Rooms were used for leisure games such as billiards, but in more recent years were converted to Norton's Car Showrooms. The Hereford registered motorcar CJ 340, halfway up the street, waits for the procession to pass. Behind the band come the local scout troop, followed by the dancing pierrots and a long trail of horsemen of varying descriptions. Again, everyone appears to be dressed up for the occasion.

BROAD STREET ON SHOW DAY   1913

Broad Street nears full capacity as the crowd streams down to the showground. The scene is a milliner's dream! Try and find anyone without a hat! The motorised open carriage to the left has stopped to allow the ladies to step down, whilst the verandah of the Norton Arms, again to the left, provides a superb vantage point from which to watch the proceedings. Stalls have been erected all around the Clock Tower at the top of the street.   Robert Newton Heyworth's studio was at No 21, near the Union Jack on the right.

THE SHOWGROUND ON SHOW DAY   1906

Robert Newton Heyworth, newly arrived in Knighton, must have been shocked to see the sleepy market town come alive for the Annual Show. Folks arrive from the surrounding districts to enter their fruit and vegetables, needlework and other crafts in the multitude of different classes. There were also horse competitions and a stunning carnival procession of incredibly imaginative floats. The photograph illustrates the superb location of the showground which sits snugly in the Teme Valley, with Kinsley Wood as the backdrop. The house in the foreground is The Cottage, home of Richard Green Price before he moved to Norton Manor.

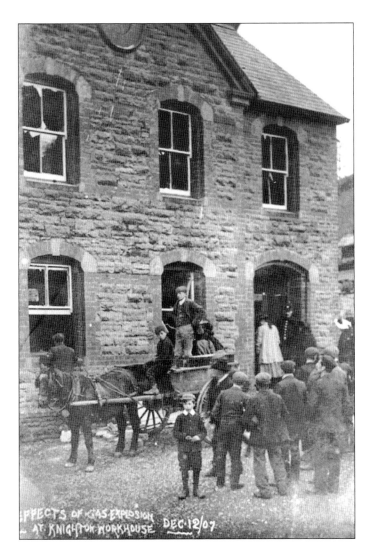

KNIGHTON WORKHOUSE – GAS EXPLOSION 1907

A small crowd has gathered outside the Workhouse, whilst the undertaker has arrived complete with coffin-laden cart. It looks ominous – and it is! Knighton Workhouse had recently had a new gas service fitted in the Receiving Room, a little distance away from the main building. At 9.30[am] on Tuesday 12th December 1907, Mr Butler, the Master, detected a smell of gas. An assistant clerk, John Jones, immediately warned the Master not to enter the room from where the smell of gas was emanating. Undeterred, Mr Butler foolishly entered the room carrying a lighted candle, obviously thinking this would help him locate the leak. Needless to say, his entry immediately triggered a terrific explosion: the build-up of escaping gas ignited. The Master was killed instantly. The roof collapsed and, as the image shows, all the windows were shattered and there was debris everywhere. None of the 64 very frightened inmates who were in fairly close proximity to the blast were injured. The explosion was heard throughout the town, and many nearby houses were badly shaken.

KNIGHTON DETACHMENT, HEREFORDSHIRE REGIMENT TA 1911

50 proud members of the Knighton Detachment, Herefordshire Regiment TA, pose in their dress uniforms, trumpeters in the front row, with their commanding officer centre picture wearing a distinctive old-style helmet. Who was to know that three years later, many of these men would be boarding a train at Knighton Railway Station, having received the call to play their part in the fighting of World War I? Mr Gwyther, the shoemaker in the Square, made and donated a pair of leather boots for every soldier who left on that train in August 1914.

THE RAILWAY STATION – TERRITORIALS AWAIT THEIR TRAIN 1914

On 4th August 1914 Belgium was invaded. At midnight on the same day Great Britain declared war on Germany. The following day these local lads, all Knighton and District Territorials, stepped aboard a train at Knighton Station on their way to their HQ Depot at Hereford. They were all members of the 1st Battalion, Herefordshire Regiment. After one year's intensive training, those that were willing to serve overseas (most were) found themselves landing at Suvla Bay as part of the ill-fated Gallipoli Campaign. 800 men in strength and serving within 53rd Welsh Division, the Regiment was forced into retreat due to intense resistance from the Turks, who were entrenched in pre-prepared and near-impregnable positions. The Herefords, at the time of their withdrawal, were only 100-strong and were promptly sent to Egypt to recuperate and await reinforcements.

The Regiment then took part in the three Battles of Gaza, the Battle of Rumani (July 1916) and the Battle of Tel Azur (Spring 1918). From the summer of that year they were to find themselves on the Western Front where they fought at the 3rd Battle of Ypres and at the horrors of the Marne. Quite a record for volunteer part-time soldiers! The survivors returned to Hereford on 23rd May 1919. It is more than likely that very few of the soldiers standing on that platform in August 1914 actually survived the conflict unscathed. The facts are these: the Herefords were to lose 227 officers and 495 other ranks; 46 officers were wounded, as were 974 other ranks. Many of these men would have been from other areas of the country, not just Herefordshire, Radnorshire and Shropshire – replacement drafts could have been from any unit. The photograph is a poignant memorial to those members of the regiment who failed to return.

ROBERT NEWTON HEYWORTH'S SHOP 1932

Seen displaying his pictures in the bay window at 21 Broad Street on left of picture.

THE RAILWAY STATION, GOODS YARD 1919

Everyone, except the horses, dutifully pose for this delightful Heyworth snapshot in the station yard. Waggoner John Davies is shown standing holding the reins of his four-in-hand as he waits for his next delivery to be loaded. Arthur Taylor, signalman, and Albert Powis, goods clerk, and an unknown railway employee complete the picture. All were employees of the London and North Western Railway Company. Upon John the Dray's retirement, his position was taken by Isaac Marsh, who used a brand-new lorry.

At a distance of some 14 miles south of Shrewsbury, the Shrewsbury and Hereford Railway Company's line reached Craven Arms. From here a new junction was formed for the Knighton Railway, the first and most northern section of the Central Wales route. At Knighton, the River Teme was diverted in order to allow for the new accommodation works to be better positioned. Lady Jane Walsh, wife of Sir John Walsh, MP for Radnorshire, cut the first sod on 19th August 1858, and the new station was opened on 6th March 1861. Knighton Station is actually in Shropshire, the diverted River Teme a little to the south being the national boundary!

Two of the businesses that would rely upon John the Dray for their deliveries.

KNIGHTON RED CROSS HOSPITAL   1914

This extensive building was constructed in 1792 as a workhouse catering for the paupers of the district. In 1834 the Poor Law Amendment Act was passed by Parliament, and subsequently the building became known as the Knighton Union Workhouse. It served 16 parishes including some in Herefordshire and Shropshire. In 1837 extensions were added at a cost of £1,800, ultimately providing facilities for 120 inmates. The principle behind such institutions was to provide food and shelter for those who were destitute; in return, inmates were expected to carry out certain tasks. Many were itinerants, moving regularly from one institution to another, there being a chain of these early work hostels along the English/Welsh border from Forden to Bishop's Castle and on to Knighton. The system operated nationwide. It was usually a good day's walk between each establishment. At the outbreak of World War I the buildings were taken over, at least in part, by the Red Cross for use as an auxiliary hospital to treat and care for wounded soldiers. At the conclusion of hostilities and having reverted back to civilian use, it had by 1920 been renamed Offa's Lodge Poor Law Institution; in 1930 it became the Public Assistance Institution, and in 1948 Knighton Hospital. Sad to relate, this is where Robert Newton Heyworth was to spend his last days before his untimely death in 1935. The hospital continues to serve the surrounding district today.

KNIGHTON RED CROSS HOSPITAL   1914

Nursing staff and wounded Belgian soldiers pose for the camera in the grounds of the former workhouse, which had been taken over for the duration of World War I for use as a Red Cross Auxiliary Hospital. The ratio of sick patients to nursing staff seems to be a little disproportionate! Dr Graves is seated in the centre of the front row, next to the Commandant (Matron), Mrs Coltman-Rogers from Stanage Park. The nurses would have been volunteers from the town and surrounding villages, and many would initially have had little or no nursing experience. It would have been a case of learning on the hoof. By 1914, there were 2,500 of this type of establishment in Great Britain, not all run by the Red Cross; they were in the main situated in large town houses or country mansions.

VISIT OF GUSTAV HAMEL, PIONEER PILOT   1913

Gustav Hamel was the son of another Gustav, a German-born royal physician, who had adopted British citizenship. The elder Gustav had always been disappointed that his son had not followed him into medicine. The younger Gustav was educated at Westminster School and Eton College.   In 1910, at the age of 21, he learned to fly at the Bleriot Flying School at Pau, south-west France. On 9th September 1911, flying a Bleriot monoplane, he flew from Hendon to Windsor (a distance of 21 miles) in ten minutes and in so doing delivered the first official airmail for the Postmaster General. He subsequently toured many parts of the country giving displays and demonstrations. He visited Monkmoor Aerodrome, Shrewsbury, in 1912. He dropped in at various shows along the English/Welsh border including Wrexham, Whitchurch, Shrewsbury, Knighton and Llandrindod Wells. This image shows Hamel's visit to Knighton on 29th August 1913 when he landed his aeroplane on an eight-acre field adjoining the showground. Sadly, on a return flight from Paris in a new 80 hp Morane-Sauliner monoplane, he mysteriously disappeared over the English Channel on 23rd May 1914.

FUNERAL OF SIR FRANCIS EDWARDS   1927

The funeral procession of Sir Francis Edwards winds its way from the church in May 1927. Always known locally as just plain Frank, he was born at Llangollen in 1852 and educated at Shrewsbury School, later becoming Liberal MP for Radnorshire 1892-95, 1900 and 1910-1918. He resided at The Cottage in Knighton for many years and was High Sheriff of the County in 1898 and was created a Baronet in 1907. Photographer Heyworth was doubtless specifically waiting for the gentleman at centre front to come along. David Lloyd George must have thought highly of his fellow MP, so much so that he journeyed to the Welsh Borders to attend his funeral. Lloyd George was born in Manchester in 1863 and after training as a solicitor at Porthmadog, he joined the Liberal Party and was elected MP for Caernarvon in 1890, becoming the youngest Member of the House, by a majority of only 18 votes. He was Prime Minister from 1916 until 1922 and died at Ty Newydd, Llanystumdwy, in 1945.

7.2 Stanage – Humphrey's Handiwork

STANAGE PARK   1925

Situated three miles from Knighton, Stanage was originally built in the 16th and 17th centuries, quite possibly for the Cornewalls, Barons of Burford, near Tenbury Wells, as a grand hunting lodge. It is known that Sir Robert Harley of Brampton Bryan lived at Stanage in the 17th century; however, by the late 18th century the property was owned by the Johnes family of Croft Castle in North Herefordshire, and it was they who demolished the old house. The present house dates from 1807 and was based on a design proposed to the then-owner, James Rogers, by the eminent landscape designer Humphrey Repton. It may seem strange having *an improver of the landscape* employed as an architect, but apparently Repton preferred to have a say in the positioning of any house on a given site before producing the garden design. A constraint guaranteed to upset any architect worth his salt! Though Humphrey Repton was known to have dabbled in architecture, in the case of Stanage, there is little doubt that he turned to one of his sons, John Adey Repton, who was an architect, to at least work up the initial thoughts – cut-out sketches provided by his father.

It is generally acknowledged that Stanage was Repton's most successful Welsh commission. It would seem that the lower portions of this Elizabethan-style house, the battlemented towers and gateways, together with the numerous stepped gables, are the realisation of Humphrey's ideas. The informal, asymmetrical groupings continued in 1822, when John Adey Repton provided more spacious rooms to the north, again in the favoured Tudor style – all towers and chimneys, the accommodation included a library and a much-admired larder-cum-dairy with pinnacles and a pyramidal roof.

The Shrewsbury architect Edward Haycock (1791-1870) was next on the scene: in 1845 he added a porch, yet more turrets and a large dining room with church-like stained-glass windows; the latter should come as no surprise since Haycock was primarily a church architect. The interior of the house is dominated by the big cantilevered staircase with a lantern above; this can safely be attributed to Edward Haycock. Humphrey Repton's work in the park includes a long tree-lined driveway, a large ornamental pond fed by a small stream, and a roadside lodge on the Knighton road which includes yet more Tudoresque touches with a loggia and four arches. Between 1807 and 1809, a wide variety of trees – some 65,000 in all – were planted, including a two-mile long reception avenue. The Coltman-Rogers family have been in residence here from about 1900.

The name 'Stanage' is thought to derive from 'Stoney Edge'. Tradition has it that Vortigern, King of the Britons in AD 455, is buried in the grounds of Stanage. In 1985, a television film called *A Blot on the Landscape,* starring George Cole, was filmed here.

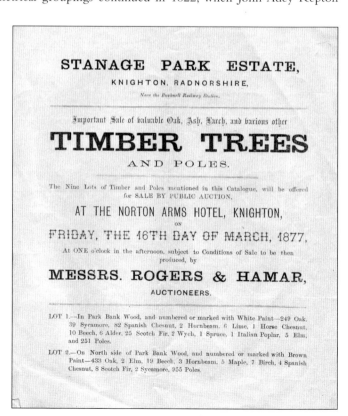

'RIDING TO HOUNDS'   1908

Rural serenity! A lady, no doubt of some local standing, ambles through the park on her trusty grey, on her way to a meet of the local hunt at Stanage. She appears to be in no rush and surely does not intend to keep up with the hounds, not if she continues to ride side-saddle, as shown? The image epitomises the unhurried pre-World War I way of life. The walled garden and greenhouse can be glimpsed through the trees on the right.

MEETING OF THE LOCAL HUNT   1908

The Radnorshire and West Herefordshire Hunt meet at Stanage Park. The mounts of the master, whipper-in, huntsmen and local dignitaries, plus a young lady on her favourite pony are all in position for Mr Heyworth's camera. The lady shown riding through the park in the previous snapshot stands immediately behind the pony club girl – she did eventually get there! The meet was usually supported by the local gentry, likely to include the Ripleys of Bedstone, the Green Prices of Norton, the Harleys of Brampton Bryan and the Coltman-Rogers family of Stanage; in addition, invited guests would normally include tenant farmers. The 2,388 acres of estate parkland, adjoining farms and undulating wooded countryside were perfect hunting ground for both fox and deer. This inviting area was also good shooting country and once offered woodcock and hare as likely rewards. Folklore relates the story of an estate gamekeeper named Price who ate the flesh of eagles, and as a result anyone who touched any of his descendants over three generations would automatically be cured of shingles. The story does not reveal where the eagles were encountered! Were there ever eagles in the Teme Valley?

7.3 Knucklas and Heyope – A Railway Landscape

KNUCKLAS ROAD, THE TOLLGATE   1906

Tollgate keeper, Mrs White, watches out for customers outside the north tollgate on the Knucklas Road at the bottom of Conjurer's Patch. Or, did she just want her photograph taken? She lived in Rose Cottage on the left, one of the very last thatched properties in Knighton when it was demolished in the 1930s. All passing vehicles and animals had to pay a toll which was utilised by the turnpike to ensure that the highway was kept in good condition. There were five roads leading out of Knighton and each one had its own tollgate. The charges were: a horse, a penny halfpenny; a wagon, fourpence per horse; pigs, fivepence per score; a gig, sixpence per horse; cart, fourpence per horse; and asses, a halfpenny each. Tollgates were closed at 10pm each evening. Incidentally, from 1794 a horse-drawn carriage travelled once a week from Knighton to London; the cost was two guineas for an inside seat and 23 shillings outside, open to the elements.

KNUCKLAS – THE CASTLE INN   1924

A youngster has been left in charge of the horse and cart whilst the driver quenches his thirst. Did he get to wet his whistle with a ginger beer by way of reward? With fancy patterned barge-boards and an unusual first-floor bay window, the inn looks to be circa 1830 in character, although it is thought a building existed here in the 17th century. George Deakin and his wife Margaret looked after the customers in 1881, and also found time to manage a farm. Margaret was the daughter of the landlord of The Ship and Castle, just two doors away, and family members continued to look after necessities until the 1980s. The Ship and Castle is reputed to have been the birthplace of Vavason Powell, the Welsh non-conformist leader and writer, who became the Ecclesiastical Governor of the border region under the Long Parliament in the 1640s.

THE VIADUCT AND CASTLE HILL   1925

An inviting view of the fertile and wooded Heyope Valley, and a dramatic setting for an elegant railway viaduct of 13 arches, each of 30-foot span, with twin-battlemented towers at each end, which was built for the Central Wales Railway in 1863 under the supervision of Henry Lote, who was primarily a church architect, a fact which goes some way to explaining its generally Gothic style. The viaduct is 190 yards in length, and the tallest arch is 75 feet above the valley floor. It is rumoured that its construction was aided in no small measure by using stone garnered from the ruins of the castle built by Hugh Mortimer II in 1225 on nearby Castle Hill, which can be seen in the background.

KNUCKLAS RAILWAY STATION AND VIADUCT   1928

A railway buff's dream! Knucklas Station platform is shown in the foreground, with the viaduct in the distance. On the 20-mile stretch from Knighton to Llandrindod Wells, the station was built by the Central Wales Railway Company. The first few miles as far as Knucklas were completed in 1861; formal opening of the section to Llandrindod Wells followed in October 1865. The station at Knucklas was originally just a timber shelter, and even the more permanent building provided later by the London and North Western Railway Company was little better, being mainly of slatted timber with brick foundations. It became an un-staffed request halt on 6th September 1965, a situation that still pertains. Intending passengers are advised: Just stick your arm out and the driver will stop. Currently, there are four trains per day each way on this Heart of Wales route, and approximately 4,000 passengers are carried each year.

HEYOPE VALLEY AND CHURCH   1912

The parish church of St David, three miles north-west of Knighton, is situated on the flat valley floor which is dissected by a minor tributary of the Teme. The church was built in 1882, under the direction of architect J L Pearson, on the foundations of a single-chamber medieval church. Simple in design, the old Perpendicular-style windows were re-used, as was the chancel screen. The west tower, topped by a shingled broach spire, is quite a landmark, visible for a considerable distance across the valley. The font is 15th century, and there is no church furniture. Heyope is infamous for the longest-burning tyre fire in the United Kingdom; it started in 1989 and lasted for 13 years until 2001.

7.4 Lloyney – Teme Valley Tranquillity

LLOYNEY, UNDERHILL   1915

This photograph highlights Underhill, the top and bottom row of cottages within the hamlet of Lloyney, situated on the banks of the Upper Teme, three miles north-west of Knighton. Nearby was once a smithy, a carpenter's and wheelwright's shop, village stores, water mill, chapel and even a tailor's premises. A wealth of different artisans and tradesmen were able to make a living in what was, even a century ago, a sparsely-populated district. Furthermore, the hamlet was virtually self-sufficient as regards everyday needs as a direct result of the labours of these individuals. How things have changed! The Builder's Arms has been renamed The Lloyney Inn and remains open.

7.5 Beguildy and Felindre – Challengingly Scenic

BEGUILDY VILLAGE   1919

Situated on the upper reaches of the Teme, eight miles from Knighton on the road to Newtown, Beguildy is a remote village set amongst hills rising to the 400-metre contour. The name means 'shepherd's home or house': an apt description, for this is sheep-rearing country. The former Oxford Arms now calls itself Church Cottage and is a private residence. The other inn, The Radnorshire Arms survives but, as with most isolated villages, Beguildy has lost its other services. Much remains of the original fabric of the 15th century parish church of St Michael. The chancel to this single-chamber church was restored in 1885; the west tower had collapsed and was replaced with a triple bell-cote in 1896 when the nave restoration was completed. The east window of three lights is of the early 15th century, as are the windows in the north and south chancel and the imposing arch-braced roofs with their tie-beams and wind-braces. One mile south of the village is a timber-framed house, the main room of which occupies the full height of the building. This is Bryndraenog, a rare and enduring survivor from the 16th century; the hall interior is spectacular, having three huge cruck trusses. John Du (Black Jack) was born at Beguildy in 1527. He was appointed Royal Tutor of Mathematics to Elizabeth I, later becoming a distinguished scientist and astronomer.

FELINDRE, WELCOMING HOME CEREMONY   1919

The caption reads: *Soldiers Welcome Home 4.8.1919.* For what is a small hamlet, a large crowd has gathered to mark the return of local heroes from the trenches of Flanders and France. Presumably, once they had touched the finishing line, returning soldiers would well and truly know that they were back amongst family and friends, once again part of the community that they had left several years previously. The gentleman to the left, just behind the rope, appears to have his welcoming speech at the ready, clutching his notes in his hand. Refreshments for everyone would no doubt have been provided, perhaps in the Wesleyan Chapel seen in the background. This celebratory occasion would have been preceded by thanksgiving hymns and prayers for the safe return of loved ones.

Imagine Heyworth peering over a hedge and setting up for these overviews of *(top)* Knighton, *(centre)* New Radnor and *(bottom)* Presteigne.

Chapter Eight

The Hundred of Radnor

Cascob
Norton
New Radnor
Walton
Evenjobb
Presteigne

8.1 Cascob – Medieval Outpost

CASCOB, ST MICHAEL   1907

Situated five miles from Presteigne and within the small community of Whitton, this little church dedicated to St Michael and All Angels dates back to the 14th century, but there may well have been an even earlier building on the site. The large circular graveyard suggests a very ancient foundation. Erected on a significant knoll, the church has a rectangular tower with a timber-framed bell section. Restored in 1895, more work is now required to the fabric: the building currently looks a little worse for wear. The place name probably derives from the hamlet's position overlooking the Cas Brook, a small tributary of the Lugg. The Rev W J Rees was rector here for 50 years until 1855 and he, together with others, has been credited with the revival of the Welsh National Eisteddfod.

8.2 Norton – Ancestral Home of the Green Price Family

NORTON MANOR   1906

Norton Manor is a large Jacobean-style house built on the site of an earlier, smaller dwelling. The latter building was in a neglected state when Richard Price, born in 1774 in Knighton, acquired the property and commissioned a new mansion which was completed in 1858. Richard Price was MP for Radnorshire from 1799 to1847 and a Lieutenant Colonel commanding the Radnorshire Militia. He died a bachelor at the age of 88 in 1862, leaving his estate to his nephew, Richard Green, who was then working in Knighton as a solicitor and living at The Cottage. Possibly as a condition of the will, but more probably out of deep gratitude to his uncle, he changed his name to Richard Green Price. The Manor has recently been subject to complete restoration and is now a country hotel with chalets and caravans in the grounds.

NORTON PARISH CHURCH (1)   1921

St Andrew's Church at Norton is essentially a Victorian rebuild of a small 15th or early-16th century edifice which had been poorly maintained for centuries. The renowned English Gothic Revival architect, Sir George Gilbert Scott, was given the commission to update the neglected church. In 1868 he added the north and south transepts to a much-restored chancel and nave, little attempt being made to replicate the original ribbed ceiling over the choir and low screen. The attractive west bell-turret is of two stages with a shingled spire; it is 17th century work.

NORTON PARISH CHURCH (2)   1921

Richard Green Price had assumed the role of Lord of the Manor in 1862, and it was he who set about organising the finance for the significant 1868 George Gilbert Scott restoration project. Only the nave was to escape major change, and it is in this area that medieval stonework survives. The much-altered screen has some original carving of the 15th century, and the font is also of this period. The reredos and pulpit are both early 20th century work.

THE SIR RICHARD GREEN PRICE MEMORIAL   1917

Following the death of Sir Richard Green Price in 1887, at the age of 84, this memorial obelisk was erected on the grassy slopes of Hawthorn Hill alongside Offa's Dyke and overlooking the minor road from Knighton to Norton and Presteigne. The monument, unveiled in December 1889, was paid for by public subscription and acknowledges Price Green's outstanding contributions to the community. Born in Madley, Herefordshire, he moved to Knighton after qualifying as a solicitor; and in 1862, after the death of his uncle, took up residence at Norton Manor. His first wife died, and he later remarried. He had 15 children, but three died in early childhood. He was responsible for the enlargement of the Norton Estate to 9,000 acres. Sir Richard led a varied and full life and was considered a pioneer in the introduction of social reforms, all of which he initiated for the benefit of his constituents. He was also, along with others, instrumental in bringing the railways to the area; and he represented both the old Radnor Borough and the County of Radnor as their MP from 1862 to 1869, and from 1880 to 1885.

The image of the obelisk reproduced above provides an excellent example of Robert Newton Heyworth's photographic skills: the focus is so sharp that one can actually read the major part of the inscription; the lines near the base of the monument are a little less clear, having become weather-worn over the years.

8.3 New Radnor – Former County Town – Maesyfed

FROM CASTLE HILL   1914

In 1536, New Radnor became the county town of Radnorshire, but it was to lose this status to Presteigne in the early 19th century. Its erstwhile distinction is surprising, considering that the town never appears to have had a sizeable population – certainly not sufficient to warrant it being the seat of regional administration. It is difficult now to appreciate that this quiet community was once so important in Welsh history. The 11th century castle, of which only the prominent mound remains, overlooks the locality it once protected. It was an important fortress during the numerous clashes involving the Welsh princes, and was not finally destroyed until the bloody altercations of the English Civil War, when Parliamentarian Forces sacked it in 1644. The hip-roofed, chimney-less building on the right-hand side of the main street is the Old Town Hall and Court. Nextdoor is The Radnor Arms which dates back 300 years and is now the only inn of an original seven still functioning. The tall memorial to Sir George Cornewall Lewis can be spotted in the background. His family seat was at nearby Harpton Court.

THE PARISH CHURCH OF ST MARY   1914

Situated just below the castle mound and perched on a terraced bank overlooking its flock, St Mary's replaced an early medieval church. Built by Thomas Dashwood in haphazard Gothic style in 1845, it is generally considered to be totally unsuited to this ancient site. Nothing of note has survived from the earlier church. An attempt was made to improve the interior in 1964, principally in the area of the altar and apse. The altar rails are notable for having been fashioned from the former Perpendicular-style screen traceries; they are of a nice scissors pattern. The west tower houses six bells and incorporates the entrance porch. The bells were recast in 1850 in memory of Devereux Plantagenet Cockburn – quite some name! He was of the Royal Scots Greys and had died aged only 22. The church now suffers badly from damp, and efforts are currently being made to raise money for urgent repairs to the roof.

CHURCH STREET 1910

Situated over 600 feet above sea-level, the diminutive town is virtually surrounded by Knowle Hill, the Smatcher, the Whimble and the Fron, and these hills funnel prevailing south-west winds in its direction. It can be a windy place at times! A quiet interlude with not a person in sight, this picture of Church Street shows a row of terraced houses, many operating as small retail premises. The shop on the near left is that of Edward Gittoes; he sold cycles, saddles, motor oil and ladies' footwear – no doubt amongst many other items. The sign on the house to the right suggests that this property was an associated business, for it also advertises the various products sold by Mr Gittoes.

At the far end of the street were the photographic studios of William H McKaig; remarkably, he also sold and repaired bicycles! As a photographer, Mr McKaig was a competitor to our very own Mr Heyworth. He was the son of Leonard McKaig, who some years earlier had moved from London to take up the post of headmaster at the local elementary school. William was to forsake his New Radnor business at the end of the First World War and take up a position in Hereford as works manager for his friend, Alfred Watkins. Here, among his many duties, he helped develop an innovative photographic light meter. His new boss had a particular penchant for experimentation and the design of new gadgetry. William's two sisters, Gertrude and Agnes, carried on with the photographic work for several years after their brother's departure.

The Watkins BEE exposure meter invented by Alfred Watkins of Hereford and further developed by William McKaig. It was very succesfully used on Captain Scott's Antartic expedition.

THE WHIMBERRY PICKERS RETURN   1912

This scene would have been relatively common in the early part of the 20th century. Pickers organised themselves into parties and scoured favourite spots on the hillsides to harvest the whimberry crop. The group here are shown with their baskets full, having spent a back-breaking day amongst the bushes. Expectant agents would be waiting to negotiate a mutually-agreed price on what, hopefully, was a bumper crop. The whimberry season usually commenced at the beginning of August and only lasted a few weeks. Some gathered the berries by hand, whilst others combed the wiry bushes using a can with nails around its top. The idea was to get the juicy berries to fall into the improvised receptacle. There were problems with this latter method, because at the end of the day the picker had to tip the collected harvest onto a white sheet and separate the berries from the chaff – in this case, stalks, leaves, small branches and other foreign matter. It was possible for the wind to do some of the work, but much had to be done by hand in order to ensure a clean crop. This winnowing process in fact amounted to double-handling – not recommended for berries destined for human consumption, but not so critical if the crop was going to the cotton or wool dyers of Lancashire or Yorkshire.

A century ago, money earned from this harvest was a bonus for local families, and was invariably spent on extra food and clothes for the children. Surprisingly enough, whimberry pickers from a community the size of New Radnor could harvest up to two tons of berries each season. The result: an awful lot of aching backs and purple fingers. The financial return in peacetime was 6d per pound; a few years later during the First World War, 2/6d per pound could be achieved, because there was an urgent need for dye for certain military uniforms.

Weights and Measures.

Lineal Measure.

4 ins. make 1 Hand.		5½ yds. make 1 Rod,	
9 ,, ,, 1 Span.			Pole or Perch.
12 ,, ,, 1 Foot.		4 Poles make 1 Chain.	
3 feet ,, 1 Yard.		10 Chains ,, 1 Furlong	
5 ,, ,, 1 Pace.		8 Furlongs 1 Mile.	
6 ,, ,, 1 Fathom.		3 Miles ,, 1 League.	
		1·151 Miles make 1 Knot.	

A Mile varies in different countries :—

	yds.		yds.
England	1,760	Ireland & Scotland	1,984
Italy	2,025	Russia	1,167
Spain	6,600	Germany	8,239
Sweden	11,067	Hungary	9,113

France measurement is Mean League of 3,666 yds

Square or Land Measure.

144	Square Inches	= 1 Square Foot.	
9	,, Feet	= 1 ,, Yard.	
30½	,, Yards	= 1 ,, Perch.	
40	Perches	= 1 Rood.	
4	Roods	= 1 Acre.	
640	Acres	= 1 Square Mile.	

An Acre equals 4,840 Square Yards.

Troy Weight.

3·17 Grains	..	= 1 Carat.
24 ,,	..	= 1 Pennyweight.
20 Pennyweights	..	= 1 Ounce.
12 Ounces	..	= 1 Pound.
100 Pounds	..	= 1 Hundredweight.

The standard for gold coin is 22 carat, fine gold and 2 carats alloy ; for silver 11 oz. 2 dwt. silver and 18 dwt. alloy.

Apothecaries' Weight.

20 Grains	.. ..	= 1 Scruple,
3 Scruples (60 grs.)	..	= 1 Drachm,
8 Drachms (480 grs.)	..	= 1 Ounce,
12 Ounces (5,760 grs.)	..	= 1 Pound, lb.

Drugs are compounded by this weight.

Avoirdupois Weight.

16 Drams	..	= 1 Ounce (437·5 grs.*)
16 Ounces	..	= 1 Pound (lb.)
14 Pounds	..	= 1 Stone (†)
28 Pounds	..	= 1 Quarter.
112 Pounds	..	= 1 Hundredweight (cwt)
20 Hundredwts.	..	= 1 Ton.

* A grain is the same in all weights.
† Butcher's Stone is 8 lb.

By Avoirdupois are weighed the larger and coarser kinds of goods, such as groceries, cheese, butter, meat, corn, etc.

Measures of Capacity—Dry Measure.

1 Minim	=	1 Drop.
1 Dram	.. =	1 Teaspoonful.
2 Drams	.. =	1 Dessertspoonful.
4 ,,	.. =	1 Tablespoonful.
60 Minims	=	1 Dram,
8 Drams	.. =	1 Ounce.
20 Ounces	.. =	1 Pint (nearly ½ litre.)
4 Gills*	.. =	1 Pint (34·659 c. in.)
2 Pints	.. =	1 Quart (1 and one-tenth litre).
2 Quarts	.. =	1 Pottle.
4 ,,	.. =	1 Gallon (277·274 c. in.)
2 Gallons	.. =	1 Peck.
4 Pecks (8 gal.)	.. =	1 Bushel (1·2837 c. ft.)
2 Bushels	.. =	1 Strike.
3 ,,	.. =	1 Sack.
4 ,,	.. =	1 Coomb.
8 ,,	.. =	1 Quarter.
12 Sacks	.. =	1 Chaldron.
5 Quarters	.. =	1 Wey or Load (51·347
10 ,,	.. =	1 Last.

An Imperial Gallon of distilled water weighs 10 lb. Avoirdupois.

A wineglass holds about 2 oz. ; a tea-cup about 3 oz.

* In the North of England half a pint is called a gill and a true gill a "noggin."

Corn is sometimes sold by weight. The average weight of a bushel of barley is 47 lb., oats 38 lb., wheat 60 lb.

Wines and Spirit Measure.

4 Gills	..	= 1 Pint.
2 Pints	..	= 1 Quart.
4 Quarts	..	= 1 Gallon.
31½ Gallons	..	= ½ Hogshead.
63 ,,	..	= 1 Hogshead.
84 ,,	..	= 1 Puncheon.
2 Hogsheads	..	= 1 Pipe.
2 Pipes	..	= 1 Tun.

Measures of Space—Angular Measure.

60 Seconds	..	= 1 Minute.
60 Minutes	..	= 1 Degree.
30 Degrees	..	= 1 Sign.
45 ,,	..	= 1 Octant.
60 ,,	..	= 1 Sextant.
90 ,, (a right angle)	=	1 Quadrant.
180 ,,	..	= 1 Semi-Circle.
360 ,,	..	= 1 Circle.

What It Felt Like.

"Something funny here," said the dentist. "You say this tooth has never been worked on before and yet I find small flakes of gold on my instrument."
"I think you have struck my back collar stud," replied the victim

Weather Forecasts—While You Wait.

Wife : "I think, dear, if it keeps fine I shall go and do some shopping. What does the weather report say?"
Husband (hastily) : "Rain, fog, sleet, snow, and a cloud-burst expected!"

54

A VILLAGE SCENE   1914

This pastoral idyll has changed little over the last century. The partly medieval King's Arms on the left was managed by Charles and Caroline Meredith from 1890 until the 1920s. In more recent times, when Wales was dry on Sundays and one just happened to be feeling a little thirsty, it was an open secret that if one popped around the back to the cowshed, a jug of ale would miraculously appear to satisfy one's fancy. The rear of the premises also housed a small abattoir, and a sheep and cattle auction was held at the front of the premises on a Tuesday. The inn is now a private residence. The white building in the centre was The Old Oak Inn in the 16th century. The elegant Georgian property to the right is The Wayside Temperance Hotel, then run by William Shewell. The parish pump was once sited on the grass strip by the streetlamp; on this patch now stands a memorial commemorating the eight villagers who lost their lives in World War I, and the three who did not return from World War II. The track to the right leads to St Mary's Church.

WATER-BREAK-ITS-NECK 1910

This large waterfall is situated off the main road between New Radnor and the hamlet of Llanfihangel-Nant-Melan. Here, the waters of the Summergil Brook fall 76 metres to the pool below, its spray creating conditions which encourage the growth of many mosses and lichens in the highly humid atmosphere. Tradition says that Llewelyn, Prince of Wales, hid in a cave above the falls in 1280, and that a hermit later lived there in the 18th century, leaving his own brand of graffiti on the walls. In the 19th century, the area was landscaped and became a tourist attraction. There is now a car park available for visitors, and a hard-surfaced footpath to the falls.

SIR GEORGE CORNEWALL LEWIS MEMORIAL   1922

Entering New Radnor from the A44 trunk road from Kington, the traveller is soon confronted by a tall Gothic-style obelisk. It was originally destined for a position high up on Castle Hill, but the architect (John Gibbs of Oxford), the Lewis family and the local inhabitants had to settle for a more lowly position alongside one of the village feeder roads. This 77-foot high memorial to Sir George Cornewall Lewis (1806-1863), a well-respected member of a public-spirited family, was erected in 1864. The Lewis family had close connections with the borderlands for half a millennium and were responsible for building nearby Harpton Court in 1750. Sir George was perhaps the most eminent member of a distinguished family; he served as MP for both Herefordshire and the Radnor Boroughs, but he was also closely associated with the foundation of the London Library and with the management of the British Museum. However, it was his political prowess as a government minister for which he is best remembered. He served under four prime ministers: namely, Robert Peel, Lord Russell, the Earl of Derby and Viscount Palmerston. He was appointed to the following positions: Poor Law Commissioner for England and Wales (1839-47), Under Secretary of State at the Home Office (1848), Financial Secretary to the Treasury (1850-52), Chancellor of the Exchequer (1855-58), Home Secretary (1859-61) and Secretary for War (1861-63).

Perhaps not the best-loved architectural style, this Neo-English Gothic obelisk is often considered to be over-elaborate, too fussy and complex in detail for modern tastes. Notwithstanding this opinion, the memorial is presently in a sorry state, requiring total restoration at a likely cost of £30,000. Health and Safety Regulations require that it remains fenced off, preventing public access until the required work is completed.

HARPTON COURT 1913

The north wing, as shown, of this large Neo-Classical stuccoed mansion of nine bays and two storeys was built for Thomas Lewis in 1750. It was followed, circa 1810, by a south façade, equally of nine bays, of bare ashlar, but with a neat porch and full-height pilasters supporting a significant pediment. There does not seem to be any definite accreditation for this work, but it is more than likely to have been designed by the eminent architect John Nash, who is known to have carried out extensive internal remodelling at this time. The residence was the home of the Lewis family, who had considerable property holdings in the vicinity from as early as the 1550s. The greater part of the building was demolished in 1956; only the north-west wing and the stable block remain, together with the avenue and the Italianate entrance lodge on the main road. The Lewis family wielded considerable influence locally, members holding numerous positions of public importance over the years. Thomas Lewis, High Sheriff of Radnorshire in the 16th century, was possibly one of the first to fulfil such a role.

SHEEP DIPPING AND THE LAW 1924

The arm of the law was always present when the annual sheep dip was in progress. This was to ensure that the dip was properly administered and every animal correctly immersed in the trough of water mixed with organophosphates. The treatment was to prevent outbreaks of sheep scab, a very contagious disease caused by parasitic mites moving from animal to animal. These mites squirm through the wool and penetrate the skin, seriously affecting the condition of the ewes and the growth rate of lambs. Furthermore, the quality of the fleece is seriously impaired. Here the children are out in force, helping to drive the animals through the dip, a practice which would not be allowed today. It is now generally accepted that organophosphates can have serious side-effects on those coming into close contact with the chemicals. One wonders just how many times in a dipping season this particular police officer had to supervise the operation in his district? These Radnor sheep are short-limbed and low-set with speckled faces, and are closely related to both the Clun Forest and the Kerry Hill breeds.

A FOREST GLADE   1910

An excellent study of a woodland glade of spruce and larch, this forest track in Warren Wood leads through the Harley Valley to the waterfall, all part of Radnor Forest. This large area of moorland, conifers and mixed woodland, which rises to a height of almost 700 metres, is a haven for wildlife including roe deer, foxes and badgers and numerous rare birds: these include pied flycatchers, redstarts and tree pipits, as well as hen harriers, goshawks, ravens, buzzards and merlin, all of which make their home here – plus the red kite, a very welcome trespasser from the Rhayader Valley and Breconshire. The Radnor Forest is not a forest in the accepted sense; rather it fits the medieval model of a hunting ground, with a mixture of terrain including farmland. Photographer Heyworth's objective was obviously to reach and record the nearby waterfall, but having come across this spot and seen the sunlight attractively filtering through the branches, he just had to stop, set up his equipment and take this photograph.

8.4 Walton – Gateway to the Basin

THE VILLAGE   1922

Walton, situated on the A44 to Rhayader and five miles north-west of Kington, is an area full of archaeological interest with numerous tumuli, mottes, Bronze Age standing stones and barrows, plus a scattering of small 1st century AD Roman camps, and a well-preserved section of Offa's Dyke. The village is 700 feet above sea-level and is part of the Walton Basin or Radnor Valley, a wide fertile area of farmland set amongst rising hills. Stanner Rocks to the south-east are reputed to be the oldest rocks in Wales; volcanic in origin and possibly 702 million years old, they are exclusively the habitat of the yellow Radnor Lily, which is also known as the Early Star of Bethlehem (Gagea bohemica). The public house, The Crown, was managed just after World War I by Harold and Ada Hughes; alas, it is no more, for it has been refurbished and is now a Thai restaurant and takeaway. The old blacksmith's shop was behind The Crown, and latterly was equipped with petrol pumps. The area is now a car park. Buildings of interest hereabouts include the part-cruck Walton Court, the 17th century Hindwell Farmhouse where Wordsworth once stayed, and the part-Regency Womaston House.

DOLYHIR QUARRY (OLD RADNOR)   1914

At the time of this photograph quarrying of these old Pre-Cambrian rocks was being carried out on a small scale. Then owned by the Old Radnor Trading Company, the quarry was eventually to pass into the hands of Tarmac Western Ltd. Situated off the B4594, on the east side of Gore Hill and 800 feet above sea-level, these hard-wearing rocks have been used over many decades primarily to provide high-grade roadstone for the highways of Radnorshire and neighbouring counties.

The mineralogy of Dolyhir Quarry is of much interest: it contains two rather unusual deposits for this district. Firstly, Ewaldite, a rare mineral, was discovered in the Yat Wood formation (on the north face of the quarry); its micro-crystals are cream in colour and hexagonal in shape. Secondly, Greenockite, a bright yellow crystal with 3mm size cleavages, was found here embedded in Sphalerite (zinc ore) and Galena (lead ore) in specific isolated limestone-based veins.

8.5 Evenjobb – Mynor Legacy

EVANCOYD, ST PETER'S CHURCH   1913

Evancoyd and Evenjobb are now as one, the population being mainly at Evenjobb which is four miles west-south-west of Presteigne. In the 19th century this rural area formed part of the Mynor Estate, the Mynor family living at Evancoyd Court. The hamlet, situated at the northern end of the Walton Basin, has lost its school, shop and most recently its post office. The Parish Church of St Peter was built to a design by T H Wyatt in 1870; externally, its prominent feature is the tower and broach spire, but the building is not generally considered to be of any great architectural merit. As is common in this district, there are numerous tumuli, a castle ring, a motte to a 12th century castle, and a well-defined surviving section of Offa's Dyke. Hereabouts, trotting races are popular and are held two or three times each year.

8.6 Presteigne – Untarnished Townscape

HIGH STREET, LOOKING EAST   1914

Presteigne is very much a small, unspoilt, border market town, its ambience retaining a definite English feel. So much so, that without resorting to maps and boundaries, it could easily be thought to be in Herefordshire or Shropshire. Formerly known as the King's Highway, this view looks towards the town centre. The shops on the right are amongst the oldest survivors in the town, for the buildings on the left were all rebuilt after the great fire of 1681. The former Market Hall at the end of the street was later to be used as a fire station; it is now the town's branch library. The roof cupola was removed in 1948 for safety reasons.

CORTON HOUSE 1915

Situated on the north-west periphery of town, this estate was owned by Sir Francis and Annie Evelyn over many decades, including at the time of this picture. Family members were renowned top-class sportsmen; one was capped for Wales at football when England were beaten 4-0 at the Oval – this must have been in the late-Victorian era. Several were competent cricketers and played at county level. The Evelyn family were also founder members of Presteigne Golf Club. In the early days, Corton was the site of the first tollgate going west out of Presteigne. On 29th October 1914, Corton House opened as a Red Cross Hospital; Miss Annie Evelyn, a daughter of Sir Francis Evelyn, was appointed Commandant, and Dr Lower was Chief Medical Officer. The picture below shows them all posing for Heyworth. There were 28 beds and six emergency beds available, and 760 patients were treated. The staff included 18 VAD nurses, and it would appear that the establishment specialised in treating soldiers requiring artificial limbs, of which 261 were fitted during the war period. Miss Annie Evelyn was later awarded an OBE for her good work.

BROAD STREET   1914

From the Victorian red-brick market hall to the delightful 17th century pack-horse bridge, this long and wide street is full of interest. The parish church of St Andrew, its churchyard, the former vicarage and the old tithe barn all hug the River Lugg and the national boundary. The group of timber-framed houses of the 16th and 17th centuries, of which Well House is perhaps most pleasing to the eye, do much to sustain the visitor's attention as he or she wanders up the street in a south-westerly direction towards the town centre. Shrewsbury architect Edward Haycock's imposing neo-Classical Shirehall of 1829, with its stuccoed finish, reminds us that this town was an important administrative centre for Radnor County from the 16th to the 20th century. The building was later used as the judge's lodgings, but now houses an interesting museum. The adjacent Red House, with its 18th century façade, deserves mention; it was the home of Rear Admiral Peter Puget from 1806 to 1812. Puget Sound, south of Vancouver Island but in Washington State, USA, is named after this naval gentleman. It is a natural area of deep water with fine harbours, and adjoins the city of Seattle. The Duke's Arms, with its 17th century galleried wing, takes its name from the Duke of Chandos, who was at various times Lord Lieutenant of Herefordshire and Radnorshire. Here was the staging post for the coach route to Aberystwyth.

THE RAILWAY STATION 1916

A delightfully sentimental scene from the era of steam! Gas lighting and enamelled advertisements are in evidence, whilst a 0-4-2 tank locomotive stands ready to depart on the branch line service to Kington and Leominster. Situated five miles and 22 chains from Titley Junction, the first sod was cut on 4th January 1872 by Miss Edith Green Price deputising for her indisposed mother, Lady Green Price of Norton Manor. The contractor was Perry and Co, of Bow, East London. The solidly-built station is of Nash Quarry limestone, with superior Bath stone for the finer detail. The overall cost was £50,750.

The branch line had been completed as far as Kington in 1857, and the extension to Presteigne was opened on 9th September 1875, a day when the celebrations were to involve the whole of the town. A procession headed by the band of the Radnorshire Rifle Volunteers was followed by numerous floats loaded with food and other everyday necessities which were distributed to the poor of the town, each family having already received a 'ticket of qualification'. This charity distribution is indicative of the social conditions prevailing in the area at the time. Shirehall was the scene of the next stage of the ceremonies, the parade eventually occupying the length of Broad Street. The gathering to meet the special train and its dignitaries included various local societies: the Oddfellows and the Foresters, the Tradesmen's Guilds, children from the Sunday schools of parish church and non-conformist chapels, and from the local elementary school, and many townsfolk. Sports events and a firework display concluded the day's extravaganza.

Presteigne Station was kept particularly busy with bulk deliveries of coal, lime and animal foodstuffs; and by the turn of the century an auction yard, adjacent to the goods shed, had been built to cater for weekly cattle markets. However, passenger numbers were never great, and as early as February 1951 the passenger service was suspended, ostensibly due to the coal shortage (a decision made permanent at the year end). Nevertheless, the busy freight traffic continued and remained in operation until 28th September 1964, albeit on Tuesdays and Thursdays only.

Time-table of the Presteign Railway, 1875					
Kington:	6.50	10.15	11.17	3.30	6.55
Titley arrive:	6.54	10.20	11.22	3.34	6.59
depart:	6.55	10.30	11.25	3.35	7.00
Presteign:	7.10	10.45	11.40	3.50	7.15
Presteign:	7.15	11.00	11.45	4.20	7.23
Titley arrive:	7.20	11.15	11.59	4.34	7.37
depart:	7.30	11.22	12.00	4.35	7.40
Kington:	7.35	11.27	12.05	4.40	7.45

Time-table of Presteign Railway, 1922			
Kington:	10.30	1.09	5.22	6.42*
Titley arrive:	10.34	1.13	5.26	6.46
depart:	10.36	1.16	5.28	6.48
Presteign:	10.48	1.30	5.40	7.00
Presteign:	10.55	2.43	6.03	7.10*
Titley arrive:	11.09	2.57	6.17	7.24
depart:	11.17	3.02	6.18	7.25
Kington:	11.21	3.06	6.22	7.29

* Wednesdays only
No Sunday Service

THE RADNORSHIRE ARMS HOTEL   1919

This property, in the upper High Street, was first built as a private residence in the 1560s, and was the home for several years of Sir Christopher Hatton – lawyer, politician and rumoured suitor of Queen Elizabeth I, the Virgin Queen. The Queen personally appointed him Lord Chancellor of England in 1587. He died in 1591. He was known as 'the dancing chancellor', a nickname alluding to his graceful dancing at court masked balls. The house was later purchased by a local man, John Bradshaw, a prominent judge on the English Circuit. It was he, together with 134 other judges, who sat at the trial of Charles I, and having passed the death sentence on the King was known thereafter as the Regicide Judge or Regicide Bradshaw. He died in 1659 and is buried in Westminster Abbey. In the 18th century, this imposing close-studded house with diagonal stone chimney stacks became known as The Cross House, simply because it stood next to the town cross. A wealthy landowner, Sir

Henry Vaughan, who was later to be arrested for committing unnatural and repugnant acts, purchased the property. He was pulled from the house and killed by the mob.

In 1792, the property became a hotel and major posting house. An increase in custom, mainly due to the coaching era, was to result in the provision of additional bedroom accommodation. In 1927, part of the building collapsed, killing 14 people. The hotel's ill-fated reputation continued when, in 1932, a windmill in the grounds burnt down and a young farmhand, Bobby Millichamp, was tried and hung for the crime of arson. However, it was later proved that he was innocent. Four years later in 1936 his brother Arthur was tried, found guilty and hanged for the same offence. Today, the premises flourish as a well-run family hotel, albeit with plenty of stories to be told! The trumpeters and escorted limousine in the photograph present a puzzle. Maybe the occasion has something to do with a visit by an Assize Court Judge!

HEREFORD STREET   1919

A two-way street, but transport of the day consisted of one wheelbarrow in each direction! The British Elementary School of 1868 is pictured on the left. It had accommodation for 100 pupils and was to come under the control of the Radnorshire Education Authority in 1906. The adjacent Baptist Chapel was built in 1845 with seating for a congregation of 260; it proved so popular that it was extended in 1885 and a schoolroom added. The black-and-white timber-framed property to the right is Cromwell Cottage and dates from 1650. The inn sign on the right behind the streetlamp advertises The Barley Mow. From 1860 to 1882, J H Weaver not only ran the pub but also the associated maltings and a new enterprise employing 40 people making spade handles. Frederick Hetch was the landlord at the time of the photograph; the inn is now closed.

THE OLD RECTORY AND CHURCH   1906

The old rectory was the home of Dr Debenham and his sister. Miss Debenham, seen in the doorway, was responsible for the establishment of the Diamond Jubilee Boys' Club in 1897. Dr Debenham stands by the greenhouse, no doubt issuing instructions to his gardeners; he was one of the first inhabitants of the town to purchase a motorcar, in 1906. At this time, the law restricted the speed of these new contraptions to 12 miles per hour, but at least the law requiring a man to walk in front of the vehicle had been repealed. The Old Rectory, a delightful residence largely unaltered to the present day, is of brick and was built circa 1740; its glebe once included a 15th century tithe barn. A replacement rectory was built in St David's Street in 1849.

ST ANDREW'S PARISH CHURCH   1920

The church is situated to the north of the town centre, close to the banks of the River Lugg, which here marks the border between England and Wales. Although Presteigne is in Wales, from the 13th century until the Reformation the church was the property of the Augustinian canons of Wigmore Abbey in nearby Herefordshire. It remains in the Diocese of Hereford. St Andrew's shows evidence of Saxon and Early Norman stonework, but the present church is basically of the 14th century. Architecturally it is a pleasing edifice, bright and spacious; the choir, south aisle and the Lady Chapel were enlarged in the 15th century, when the chancel was also rebuilt in Downton stone. Over the years, the building has been well maintained, with three separate restoration projects since 1855. That year the gallery over the Lady Chapel was removed. Extensive work was carried out in 1891 under the direction of J L Pearson when the stone pulpit was erected, improvements carried out to the roofs, and repairs to the nave completed. Additionally, the scheme included the provision of the ornate chancel, together with the teak screen in the south aisle and repairs to aisle windows. In 1927, Nicholson and Clarke of Hereford supervised the removal of the pews and their replacement with chairs, and the stripping of lime-based plaster from the nave and other areas.

The massive church tower houses eight bells, and its clock has been constantly chiming since 1838. The church has the only working wooden carillon of its type in Great Britain, dating back to 1726. This apparatus allows the bells to be played mechanically, usually via a keyboard. In 1737, Richard Owen of Little Brampton presented to the church a rare early-16th century Flemish woven tapestry illustrating Christ's Entry into Jerusalem. It hangs on the north wall. Also on the north wall hang the laid-up and framed battle colours of both the Radnorshire Militia and the Rifle Volunteers. Large in size and of faded silk, they date from the first quarter of the 19th century and have recently been painstakingly restored. Donations from local benefactors and an inspirational and caring congregation has allowed this lovely church to deal adequately with problems associated with the rigours of time and weather.

In the graveyard is buried 17-year-old Mary Morgan, who was hanged for the murder of her new-born child in 1805. The father of the child apparently sat on the jury but was himself involved with the crime. Strenuous local efforts were made to obtain a reprieve for Mary, and a successful journey was made to London – only for the legal documents to arrive back in Presteigne too late to be effected.

The rare 16th century flemish tapestry displayed in the church.

HIGH STREET, LOOKING EAST   1924

The Victorian Market Hall is again featured in this animated street scene which shows two early motorcars threading their way towards the cameraman. But what exactly is going on in the foreground? People are sufficiently interested to gather on the pavements, as two strong Hereford bullocks pause at the roadside. The answer is that these animals are pulling the Atora suet advertising van which toured the area publicising this particular product. The story began in 1893 when a Frenchman living in Manchester, having watched his wife laboriously chopping up suet, thought that it would be a good idea to retail ready-prepared suet. As a result his product was very soon being sold all over the world. The Atora name derives from 'toro' meaning bull. The advertising campaign started in 1923 and ran for nine years, with Sinbad and Sailor, the two bullocks, touring the country during this time. The animals were reared by William Deakin of the Gravels Farm, Downton on the Rock, Herefordshire and were trained and driven by Reginald Lippett, William Deakin's brother-in-law. Incidentally, these bullocks would have had to pay frequent visits to the farrier, as most of their walking was done on hard-surfaced highways.

HIGH STREET, LOOKING WEST   1914

Looking north-west away from the Market Hall, this portrait of High Street has changed little over the years. Of necessity, traffic is now one-way, but at the time of the photograph there was nothing much more to be seen than a few bicycles. Many of these shop fronts have survived the intervening years, but in most cases the premises have undergone a change of trade or usage. Much of what is visible is Edwardian or Victorian, with a few buildings of the Georgian era, but these frontages mask an inner soul, for the properties are timber-framed, originally constructed several centuries earlier. The sign to the right, above the youngster with his bicycle, advertises A R Davies' chemist shop. Trading here for 52 years, he later joined forces with Mr Perkins of Knighton, operating as Davies and Perkins from 1922 onwards. A Model T Ford trundles down the street, no doubt soon turning a few heads. One business which has proved invaluable to this publication is that of Ivan Monckton, situated to the left at No 45, halfway along the street: his King's Head bookshop invariably has a large collection of secondhand books, stamps, ephemera and postcards for sale!

PROSPECTING FOR COAL 1913

Geologists of the time must have harboured thoughts of finding coal in the alluvial deposits of the Lugg Valley. Over a period of several decades, numerous attempts were made to locate coal-bearing seams in the Presteigne district, none of which proved successful. In 1911, Charles Rogers of Stanage Park sunk a trial boring in Presteigne, as did a Mr Philip Davies. In the same year, Aaron Griffiths of Willey Lodge purchased 26-acre Folly Farm, quite possibly on the strength of having found a few pieces of coal lying on the surface. In 1913 he carried out trial borings at Folly Bank, illustrated, but these too were unsuccessful. The shareholders of his newly-formed Radnor Coal Syndicate, who had purchased a total of 826 shares, would not have been very pleased. Aaron Griffiths was to die suddenly of peritonitis on 23rd September 1913. Subsequently, the syndicate was wound up in November 1915, members having come to the decision that no black gold was present in the rocks of Presteigne.

PRESTEIGNE SHOW (1)   1909

This postcard was sent to Winnie Newell by her sister, Nellie. She writes: '*I thought you would like this one of the Show*'. This is the 15th Annual Show, held on the Silia Meadow on the south-west outskirts of the town; and this view is remarkable for the array of automobiles lined up along the edge of the viewing area. The white car nearest the camera is a Daimler, and there is another example a little further along. It is difficult to positively identify the other vehicles, but one is a Star, from the Wolverhampton factory. The Show Field was part of J H Wale's estate; he was a prominent local liberal and non-conformist. Silia House and gardens were laid out by an earlier owner, a Captain James Beavan who, during the 1860s and '70s, planted what are now some of the finest conifers in the country.

PRESTEIGNE SHOW (2)   1913

Another postcard to Winnie Newell, this one a delightful view of the attentive crowd watching the events at the 19th Annual Show. The large well-dressed crowd awaits further events in the parade ring. Sisters Winnie and Nellie Newell were members of the well-known family of long-established Broad Street ironmongers. The business was first established in 1770, and survived for over 200 years, closing in 1974. At one time there was a small nail factory at the back of the retail premises. When the shop closed, the entire stock was purchased by St Fagans National History Museum in Cardiff. In 1947, part of Silia Meadow was sold off for housing development; and in 1994 Silia Woods were donated to the Woodland Trust, but public access is still permitted.

MISS IDA DAVIES, AGE 7, PRESTEIGNE SHOW   1909

This is a nice example of an advertising postcard and a wonderful record of rural life a century ago. The little girl is specially dressed up for the occasion, her lace-bottomed bloomers providing the finishing touch. The machine shown was used to separate cream from the milk, and many monotonous hours turning both a separator and then a churn would be required to produce a little bit of butter. Alexander and Duncan are now large distributors of farm machinery from their depot in Leominster. The message on the back of the card tells a Mr Davies of New Radnor that *'Our Mr Owen has delivered the cord to the bottom of the lane'*, signed Alexander and Duncan, Dairy Engineers, Kington.

PUSHBALL TEAM, PRESTEIGNE SHOW   1928

A wonderful portrait of an anonymous bunch of athletic lads! Pushball was invented by M G Crane and was first played at Harvard University, Massachusetts, in 1894. The first game known to have been played in Great Britain was at Crystal Palace in 1902. The playing area was 140 yards in length, with an overall width of 50 yards; goalposts were 18-feet high with a 7-feet high crossbar, and the distance between the posts was 20 feet. The rubber ball was 6 feet in diameter and weighed 50 pounds. It had to be pushed or even carried by 11-a-side teams. The rules included five points for getting the ball between the posts, and an unlikely eight points if lifted over the crossbar. An apparently boisterous game, played by fit young lads, frequently students, with energy to spare. The game was often played at local shows and fêtes, and was especially popular at agricultural shows. It is now thought to be lost as an active sport in this country.

PRESTEIGNE
AND DISTRICT AGRICULTURAL SOCIETY.

PRESIDENT — H. Fitzherbert Wright, Esq., M.P.

THE NINETEENTH ANNUAL

SHOW

Will be held at "Silia," Presteigne, on

Tuesday, Sept. 16th, 1913.

By kind permission of J. H. Wale, Esq., and T. Lewis, Esq.

VALUABLE CUPS AND SPECIALS. **£320** IN PRIZES

HORSES, CATTLE, SHEEP & PIGS,
DOGS AND POULTRY,
PIGEONS AND RABBITS.
HORSE (Open & Local) LEAPING,
DRIVING AND SADDLE CLASSES
SHEEP DOG TRIALS.
BUTTER AND EGGS — WEIGHT JUDGING CONTESTS

TWELVE SHOWS IN ONE.
PRESTEIGNE TOWN BAND.
Public Luncheon and Tea on Show Ground.
For special Railway facilities see small Bills.
All Information from S. YOUNG, Sec., Presteigne.

Chapter Nine

The Hundred of Cefnllys

Pilleth
Llangunllo
Bleddfa
Dolau
Llandrindod/Cefnllys

9.1 Pilleth – Dispute and Conflict

PILLETH COURT AND ST MARY'S CHURCH   1914

Pilleth is mentioned in the Domesday Book, a rare occurrence for south Central Wales. It is beautifully situated on the south-west facing slopes of the Upper Lugg Valley, some five miles from Presteigne. St Mary's church shares this idyllic landscape with 17th century Pilleth Court. History tells us that it was here, on 22nd June 1402, that Owain Glyndwr, Prince of Wales, inflicted his last defeat on the King's armies led by Edmund Mortimer, Lord of the Marches. In the 19th century, the Price family of Pilleth Court are reputed to have found the burial ground where thousands of the battle casualties were laid to rest, and they subsequently planted four Wellingtonia conifers as a mark of respect. Pilleth Court is principally of the early 17th century and was probably an H-plan house, of which the north and central wings survive. It is an early example of the use of brick in the district; the chimney stacks to the north and west are original. St Mary's Church was gutted by fire in 1894, but restoration under the guidance of architect William Tapper had to wait until 1911. At that time, due to lack of funds, the roof only had basic repairs carried out, just enough to make it weatherproof. This sufficed until full restoration came in 2002 at a cost of £312,000. Its sturdy, buttressed west tower with stair turret is 14th century.

9.2 Llangunllo – Headwaters of the Lugg

THE SQUARE AND GREYHOUND INN   1912

The author's namesake, David Evans the landlord, stands on the left in this pre-war view of the 19ᵗʰ century inn. Situated on a minor road, the village has lost all its amenities; even its railway station is two miles distant. Llangunllo is a quiet spot amidst windswept countryside which can be bracing but is always robustly healthy. A long succession of landlords was to follow David Evans, including L A Davies in the 1920s and H Harrison in the 1930s; Mr Bryant, the landlord in the 1950s unfortunately fell off his donkey and was drowned in a gutter. Bill Matheson was pulling the pints here for 40 years from the 1960s. The village community shop now functions from the front room of The Greyhound.

WINTER WHITEOUT   1933

For three days from 23ʳᵈ to 26ᵗʰ February 1933, the Welsh hill country was hit by a blizzard of considerable intensity. It was to leave most of the district completely cut off, with all services coming to a total standstill. It was not possible to replenish supplies, and vehicles were unable to negotiate the four feet of lying snow and wind-blown drifts of up to 12 feet in height. Apparently, the storm was totally unexpected: many farmers were caught out and spent many hazardous hours rescuing their animals. The image shows the Lyons Tea delivery van battling against the elements at Llangunllo, where it was about to relieve five days of isolation.

9.3 Bledffa – Forest Heights

THE PARISH CHURCH   1924

Bleddfa translates as 'the place of the wolf', and tradition has it that the last wolf in Wales was shot here. The church, dedicated to St Mary Magdalene, is in the diocese of Swansea and Brecon, was built in the late 13th century and since then has suffered its share of misfortune. The original tower is believed to have been destroyed by followers of Owain Glyndwr prior to the Battle of Pilleth. Reconstruction work commenced in the 15th century, when a new chancel roof of tie-beams, king posts and braced collar beams were provided. The boarded bell-turret is of 1711. Further restoration was carried out in 1907 with the provision of a flagstone floor and replacement of stone window surrounds in the nave; this area remains partitioned, a reminder of its use as a schoolroom. The iron parish chest is from Coalbrookdale. The font is octagonal and likely to be 14th century work. In 1977 all the fittings were made moveable, an interesting attempt to encourage wider usage of the building for other purposes than church services. The register dates from 1603.

THE HUNDRED HOUSE   1926

Six miles from Knighton on the A488 road to Llandrindod Wells, this property was built in the 16th century, originally as a courthouse serving the Cefnllys Hundred. From this building criminals were pursued and apprehended, and justice administered. It is thought that the building first became an inn in the mid-19th century. At the time of this photograph the landlord was Christopher Bridgewater. The attached single-storey building nearer to the camera is believed to have been built specifically as a detention cell for workmen employed on the construction of the Rhayader to Birmingham water pipeline, who had badly misbehaved or broken the law. It was later used as the canteen/kitchen for the nearby school. The inn has recently undergone refurbishment.

9.4 Dolau – Ramblers' Paradise

DOLAU SPORTS (1)   1920

This appears to have been very much a social occasion, with everyone in the neighbourhood turning up at Tan House Chapel Field either to watch or take part in the various events – none of which were to be taken too seriously. These sports days were probably held annually over a number of years, no doubt organised by a locally-appointed committee who would select the officials and draw up a list of competitors – although it may have been acceptable for entries to be received on the day. This view of the pole vaulting is primitive by today's standards; the posts securing the bar are very utilitarian, and the competitors' attire not at all conducive to helping them clear the bar. The total absence of a soft landing area does not exactly inspire confidence. Of course, pole vaulting has its origins in the fenlands of East Anglia and also in Holland, where it was a practical means of crossing dykes or drains, often of significant width.

DOLAU SPORTS (2)   1920

The children's egg-and-spoon race nears its conclusion, but it is too early to say that the frontrunner will win. Personal experience confirms that anything can happen in the last few strides! White frocks predominate; boys are never keen on this particular race. The grass seems rather too long for serious sporting endeavour, and there seems to be a bit of cheating going on – the competitor on the left is surely holding her egg on the spoon. Instant disqualification is called for!

DOLAU SPORTS (3)   1920

Entrants line up for the 100-yards dash; two are in running kit, whilst the chap in the middle has just cast off his jacket and rolled up his shirt-sleeves. Notice that he crouches in a rather professional-looking starting pose. Perhaps he won first prize! Maybe as far as the more correctly attired competitors are concerned, it is a case of: *All the gear! No idea!*

DOLAU SPORTS (4)   1920

Situated in the River Arun Valley, Dolau is a small village close to Llanfihangel Rhydithon and six miles north-east of Llandrindod Wells. 'Dolly' to the locals, it is an ideal centre for walking and exploring the nearby Radnor Forest, particularly using the Heart of Wales railway line; the station at Dolau is welcoming, well-maintained and attractive. Here, on this postcard, spectators linger awhile and listen to the band on Sports Day in this rather secluded part of the borderlands; as usual everyone is dressed up in all their finery.

9.5 *Llandrindod Wells/Cefnllys — Victorian Spa*

THE SHAKEY BRIDGE   1912

The so-called Shakey Bridge spans the River Ithon, two miles west of Llandrindod Wells. This descriptive label was given to the original Victorian footbridge, which consisted of wooden planks and wire-rope supports. It was well used by walkers and those wishing to visit nearby Cefnllys Castle ruins, and the medieval church of St Michael. The bridge shown here has a central timber support and what appears to be a metal trough and rails, and is obviously a replacement. Further upgrading took place just prior to World War II when a steel and concrete footbridge was erected.

THE GOLF COURSE   1912

The game of golf was introduced to this spa town in 1889, when the then-owners of the Pump House Hotel appointed Alexander Patrick of the Royal Wimbledon Golf Club to develop a 9-hole golf course on what was common land adjacent to the hotel and lake. The course was closed by the town council in 1905, apparently for safety reasons. Almost immediately a syndicate of seven local gentlemen, led by cycle and motorcar dealer Tom Norton, established the Llandrindod Wells Golf Club Company and very soon leased 140 acres of land on nearby Little Hill. They appointed Harry Vardon, a former British Open Champion, to design a new golf course of 18 holes. A clubhouse was erected; on 21st May 1906 the first inter-club match was played against Newtown; and the official opening ceremony took place almost a year later, on 18th May 1907. The Club has hosted many national events over the years and in 2004 won the Welsh Club of the Year title. Would you find ladies traipsing around the local course accompanying their husbands in this day and age? The two ladies in this snapshot, suitably dressed for the weather, did not seem to mind in 1912!

THE GOLF CLUB PAVILION   1919

This timber-constructed clubhouse was supplied by the Wire Wove Company of Victoria Street, London and, following its erection on 21st May 1906, it was fully fitted-out and officially opened on 18th May 1907. In the period before the First World War, Tom Norton's converted Model T Ford bus, which he named Colonel Bogey, would take a maximum of 11 passengers to the Golf Club for the princely sum of 9d each going up, and 6d each coming down. Some passengers, who had other interests, would travel to the top of the hill and the Cairn Tea Rooms, order tea and scones, admire the views and take in the bracing air! Caddies were brought in from the orphanage at Newport, Monmouthshire and would be paid 1/9d per day. Sunday play was allowed after 1914. One club official of note was J Lewis Wilding, who retired as Secretary in 1935 after 30 years' service. Famous people known to have visited the club include David Lloyd George and Field Marshal Earl Haig. Clay-pigeon shooting was also a popular pastime of members in the early years. The old timber clubhouse had served its time by 1974, when it was demolished and replaced with a modern building.

THE PUMP HOUSE HOTEL   1912

This enterprise started from very humble beginnings way back in 1736. Mrs Jenkins, tenant of Bach-y-Graig Farm, was at this early date selling salt and sulphur spring water to visitors as a cure for their ailments. It became known as the Pump House, and it was here that the Pump House Hotel was built in 1889. Further extensions were added, and the hotel was eventually able to offer 200 bedrooms. During the Second World War the accommodation was taken over as a military hospital and as an officer training unit. The hotel re-opened for a short period after the war years, but closed in 1947, only to be re-incarnated shortly afterwards as a residential school for the deaf. It was subsequently used for several years by Powys County Council as their headquarters, but was eventually demolished circa 1989.

THE BRYNAWEL HOTEL   1911

It can come as no surprise when looking at this photograph to learn that the Brynawel has its origins in five large Victorian terraced houses, all forming part of what was South Crescent. The end result of the conversion project was a hotel providing every modern convenience, plus tennis courts, bowling greens and stabling facilities. Electric lighting was also installed. The hotel changed its name to Glen Usk immediately after World War I. Full renovation of the accommodation was undertaken in the 1980s, and this brought the hotel up to modern-day standards, with 79 en-suite bedrooms together with associated conference and function rooms.

THE HOTEL METROPOLE   1924

Edwin Coleman, a postmaster from the nearby village of Howey, opened this hotel as The Coleman in 1872. John Wilding, who also owned The Severn Arms at Talybont, took it over in 1885, at the same time changing its name to The Bridge Hotel. It was sold again in 1897 to Elizabeth Miles, who developed the complex and again renamed it in 1911, this time giving it an altogether grander title – The Metropole. Elizabeth's son, Francis, took over in 1925 and continued to expand the facilities, including the provision of a large open-air swimming pool on land immediately adjacent to the hotel. Unfortunately, the hotel fell into disrepair in the late 1930s. The army took up occupation during World War II, and the building suffered further dilapidation. A determined group of descendants of Elizabeth Miles, owner of the hotel at the turn of the century, then decided that the premises should be brought back to something like their former glory. This was achieved and the hotel continues to be managed by the same family, who have added an indoor swimming pool and a leisure centre to its attractions. The 120-bedroom Metropole is now very much the fashionable place to stay in Mid-Wales.

ROCK PARK HOTEL   1911

An 18th century thatched inn once stood on this site which formed part of the Rock House Estate, a holding offered for sale in 1867. The outcome, following the discovery of a spring, was a pump room, soon to be superseded by a new Rock Park Hotel, a facility developed by Richard Green Price of Norton Manor, near Presteigne. The natural contours of the land were developed into a landscaped rock park. Visitors are recorded as paying 6[d] per day to drink as much of the mineral-rich water as they wished, supposedly in the hope of curing their various ailments, real or otherwise! 31,000 visitors arrived to test the waters in Llandrindod Wells in 1891. The Rock Park Hotel survived a fire in 1947 and continued operating until closure came in 1995, followed by demolition in 1997. The site is now covered by housing.

GWALIA HOTEL   1924

On a prime corner site between Norton Terrace and Rock Park, the Gwalia Hotel was built in 1899, somewhat late in this spa town's rush to accommodate the Victorians' predilection for hydropathic treatments. The accommodation was always of the highest standard and very modern for the time. The revolving entrance door must have caused some amusement to many visitors, children especially. Edward Elgar and David Lloyd George, among other notables, are known to have stayed here. The army requisitioned the property during the Second World War, and it was never again to achieve its former glory. The building was purchased by Radnorshire County Council in 1951 and it continues as a seat of local government administration up to the present day. The Model T Ford standing at the kerbside is of interest, with a coat slung across the seat; it may very well belong to Robert Newton Heyworth, the provider of all the images within this publication.

EQUINE PUSHBALL - 1913

This image is fascinating and more than a little weird but, unfortunately, the precise location is not known. It could be a small arena, possibly associated with the military. Perhaps somewhere in the Llandrindod Wells district. It was normal to have six players on horseback per team, and the intention was to manoeuvre the six-foot diameter ball between your opponent's goalposts. Here, the teams take a well-earned rest at the half-time interval. The popularity of the game waned, and it was played very little after World War I, except in Holland and Germany.

Conclusion

Alas, our Border Wanderings are over. The author hopes you have enjoyed this book, and joining him and Robert Newton Heyworth on their travels through some of the most picturesque countryside in Britain. David, like Robert, visited every location featured on the postcards in this book and suggests that the reader might like to do the same.

Armed with the book, visit the lake in the lovely spa town of Llandrindod Wells, the viaduct at Knucklas spanning the Heyope Valley, and Panpunton Hill with its exhilarating views over Knighton. Take a look at the waterfall at New Radnor; wander and wonder why this was once such an important town. Do not overlook the site of the Battle of Pilleth. Journey on through the Walton Basin taking in the hamlets and villages en route to Presteigne, where you can visit the Judge's Lodgings and soak up the history of this border staging-post. Travel to Norton, Lingen and Leintwardine – all have their individual beauty, surrounded by scenery unsurpassed. Brampton Bryan, Hopton and Wigmore Castles remind us of Civil War turbulence long ago. Cast your mind back to ancient times as you climb up to Caractacus' Camp behind idyllic Chapel Lawn.

Imagine the former bustle of Bucknell Station while you sit waiting for an occasional Heart of Wales train. Seek out the isolated villages of Edgton, Hopesay and Burrington, all peace and tranquillity, remnants of real Old England. The black-and-white town of Pembridge with its medieval church and detached bell-house should not be missed, nor Bishop's Castle with its Railway Museum and pub-breweries offering a taste of English beer at its best. And then there is Church Stretton, our own Little Switzerland, with the 12-mile Long Mynd as a spectacular backdrop. Last but not least, do not neglect the gem of Shropshire: the unspoilt, undulating wooded hills of the Clun Valley, starting at Craven Arms and passing through Aston on Clun, Clunbury, Clungunford, Clunton, Clun, and on up to Newcastle on Clun. Little wonder that A E Housman was so taken with this special valley.